When Freedom Was Lost

When Freedom Was Lost

The Unemployed, the Agitator, and the State

LORNE BROWN

BLACK
ROSE
BOOKS

Montréal·Buffalo

Black Rose Books No. 0 108

ISBN Hardcover 0-920057-75-6
ISBN Paperback 0-920057-77-2

Canadian Cataloguing in Publication Data

Brown, Lorne
    When freedom was lost

ISBN 0-920057-75-6 (bound). — ISBN 0-920057-77-2 (pbk.).

1. Unemployed—Canada—History. 2. Labor camps—Canada.
3. Depressions—1929—Canada. 4. Canada—Economic conditions—1918-
1945. I. Title.

FC577.B76 1987   331.13'7971   C86-090312-5

Cover design: J.W. Stewart

Black Rose Books

3981 boul. St. Laurent   University of Toronto Press
Montréal, Qué. H2W 1Y5   33 East Tupper St.
Canada   Buffalo, N.Y. 14230, USA

Printed and bound in Québec, Canada

dedicated to my mother, Geneva Brown

"Those who profess to favour freedom, and yet depreciate agitation, are men who want crops without ploughing up the ground. They want rain without thunder and lightning. They want the ocean without the awful roar of its waters. This struggle may be a moral one or it may be a physical one; it may be both moral and physical; but it must be a struggle. Power concedes nothing without a demand. It never did, and it never will. Find out just what people will submit to, and you will have found out the amount of injustice and wrong which will be imposed upon them; and these will continue until they are resisted with either words or blows, or with both. The limits of tyrants are prescribed by the endurance of those whom they oppress...." *Frederick Douglas,* August 4, 1857

"From the point of view of the future of Canada in my opinion it is much healthier to find that twenty thousand young men are restless to the point of revolt, after having been kept in camps from one to three years, than it would be if they were content." *Agnes MacPhail, M.P.,* House of Commons, July 2, 1935

"And if you're looking for monuments to the man, go up along the CPR mainline and watch for those still standing tar papered shacks into which Bennett herded the unemployed youth of Canada back in those days. They're empty now, their windows boarded up, deserted for years. And Arthur Evans is the man who closed them down forever, so far as labour is concerned." *Charles Stewart,* at the funeral of Arthur (Slim) Evans, Leader of the On-to-Ottawa Trek, February 17, 1944

Table of Contents

Acknowledgements   11
Introduction   13
    I.   Catastrophic Unemployment   17
   II.   Promises Unfulfilled   29
  III.   The Establishment of Relief Camps   47
  IV.   Conflict in the Camps   57
   V.   The Camps as a Political Liability   83
  VI.   Mass Walkout in British Columbia and Stalemate
        in Vancouver   103
  VII.   The Struggle Escalates and the Trek Begins   125
VIII.   A Migration Unique in the History of Canada . . .   147
  IX.   Stalemate in Regina and Confrontation in Ottawa   159
   X.   The Regina Riot   179
  XI.   The Political Repercussions and the Legacy of the
        Trek   201

Acknowledgements

Much of this book is based on research I did over the years at the Public Archives of Canada, the Saskatchewan Archives, the Provincial Archives of British Columbia, and the Vancouver Public Library. The staff at these institutions were always helpful and I owe them a debt of gratitude.

Jane Broderick, editor at Black Rose Books, improved the text immeasurably by excising errors and inconsistent and redundant word usage. Emily Latimer of the University of Regina typed and retyped the manuscript with skill, stamina, and much patience.

In 1985 the Canadian Plains Research Centre at the University of Regina sponsored a conference to commemorate and examine the events surrounding the On-to-Ottawa Trek of 1935. Participants, including the author, learned first-hand about the unemployed struggles of the 1930s. Those crucially responsible for making that educational experience a success include James McCrorie, author of *In Union is Strength,* Gillian Minifie, and Terry Zimmer. At the conference I had the opportunity of meeting, hearing, and learning from several of the veterans of the Trek. They include Robert (Doc) Savage, Matt Shaw, and Robert (Bobby) Jackson. Jean Evans Sheils was also helpful in recalling many of the events associated with her father, Arthur (Slim) Evans, Leader of the On-to-Ottawa Trek. I am indebted to Bill Gilbey, one of the founders of the Relief Camp Workers' Union and a labour activist all his life, who has over the years provided me and many of my students with valuable insights into the labour struggles of the 1930s.

11

Introduction

Canadians are now living through the worst economic depression since the 1930s. The unemployment rate, even going by the very conservative official estimates, has exceeded ten percentage points for several years and is expected to do so into the foreseeable future. And official government statistics tell only a small part of the story, even in a statistical sense. They do not pretend to count the large numbers who have become so discouraged that they have ceased looking for work. Nor do they count people living on Indian reserves where in some cases unemployment is as high as ninety per cent, or the many women who would work and add a badly needed supplement to the family income if there was the slightest possibility of finding a job.

In this present depression we have long since passed the point where the so-called "safety net," established in Canada mainly since World War II, has been able to prevent widespread suffering and even malnutrition among some sectors of the population. For hundreds of thousands, unemployment insurance, inadequate as it is, has run out, and the authorities are purposely making it more difficult to obtain. Welfare, transfer payments and social services of nearly every kind are being cut back by the federal government and most provincial governments. And for those fortunate enough to be employed the real standard of living has been declining for several years.

Those who doubt the above assertions need only examine government statistics. The number of people *officially* unemployed in Canada increased by sixty-one per cent between 1981 and 1984.[1] The increase was much greater for particular regions. The number of unemployed increased by 144 per cent in British Columbia and 196 per cent in Alberta in this period.

13

That the results have meant actual want for many people can be confirmed by officials of churches, charitable organizations and municipalities who operate hostels and "soup kitchens." Further, there are now food banks in eight Canadian provinces[2]: 94 were established between 1981 and 1985. These food banks are supplementing the diets of hundreds of thousands of Canadians annually. They have become an embarrassment to our governments and have prompted some politicians to suggest they have been organized for that purpose by people with ulterior motives. The poor are expected to stay out of sight and go hungry in silence to save face for the apologists of the established system.

There are many similarities and many differences between the present depression and the Great Depression of the 1930's. The Great Depression was, of course, on a much more devastating scale. It also occurred during an era when there were hardly any social services provided by the state and when working people had few organizations to defend their interests. It is these factors which have helped to mitigate the worst consequences of the present depression for the majority of people.

The similarities between today and the 1930s are also very striking. In both instances the governments of the day have attempted to force working people, and especially the least protected and hence the poorest, to bear the brunt of the depression. The big corporations and the economic elite can thus be spared the full consequences of what they have wrought.

This is evident today with the New Right strategy of dismantling social services and limiting the state to the role of buttressing the private sector of the economy. Prime Minister Mulroney and his ministers are attempting to implement such a strategy wherever they dare and as much as they can get away with. The Social Credit government of British Columbia has been pursuing such a strategy with a vengeance, and with disastrous consequences for the province, for the past four years. Other provincial governments have been adopting similar albeit less far reaching policies and with less flamboyant overtones.

This book is about some of the consequences of a similar strategy by the Conservative Bennett government of the early 1930s under somewhat similar but at the same time very different circumstances. More specifically, it is about the single unemployed youth who were the chief victims of that strategy. It is also about their attempts to organize and the ensuing struggles between the organized unemployed and various levels of the state in Canada.

14

In many respects, the organized unemployed were the cutting edge of the major struggles of the early 1930s, which were to reach titanic proportions by 1935. It was these struggles which helped lay the basis for the organization of the great industrial unions of the late 1930s and beyond. They also played a role in forcing the business community and the authorities to move in the direction of the so-called "positive state" which eventually established unemployment insurance and a host of other institutions which working people today consider rights and are struggling to defend and enhance.

Perhaps more than anything else, this book is concerned with the strategies and resulting tactics adopted by the organized unemployed and their allies to defend their rights and to eventually force state authorities to yield to at least some of their demands. Parliamentary debates and conventional lobbying techniques played a very small role. Circumstances necessitated that the only effective strategy would have to rely on extra-Parliamentary organization and agitation. The struggles were fought out in the relief camps and in the streets, the factories, the mines, the soup kitchens, and the police stations of this country. These struggles became sufficiently disruptive that government authorities and mainstream politicians feared for the political stability of the country. The organized unemployed also enjoyed such obvious popular support that politicians could ignore their demands at their peril. Out of all this turmoil came significant and progressive social change.

The contemporary unemployed in Canada have begun to organize once again. Considerable agitation is already underway, in fact, but groups have not yet become sufficiently well organized or militant and disruptive enough to become a constant focus of national attention and concern. Politicians and state authorities therefore merely pay lip service to the plight of the unemployed. The specific issues of the struggle will differ from those of the 1930s because the circumstances and political culture have changed. What remains constant is that progressive social change will by necessity have to be preceded by agitation, organization, and militant struggle.

Footnotes

1. Graham Riches, "Food Banks and the Collapse of the Public Safety Net in Canada: Dangers and Opportunities." Paper for forthcoming issue of *International Review of Community Development*. All contemporary statistics cited in the Introduction are from Riches.
2. *Ibid.*

Camp-made violin and its maker, name unknown, Relief Project No. 57, Vancouver Island, September 1934. (Photo #36034, Public Archives of Canada)

CHAPTER I

Catastrophic Unemployment

The "roaring twenties" often referred to in our literature as a period of tremendous economic expansion and prosperity were no picnic for working people in Canada. The first half of the 1920s was characterized by agricultural depression and extremely high unemployment resulting from the economic downturn after World War I. It is little wonder that this period witnessed economic, social and political struggles on an unprecedented scale.

On the labour front there were fierce trade union struggles ranging from the Winnipeg General Strike of 1919 to the great upheavals in the Cape Breton coal fields of 1922 and 1923. Out of these struggles arose political formations which were to grow slowly throughout the 1920s and then expand and play a greater role in the great political controversies of the 1930s. On the agrarian front the rise of the farmers in politics and the building of the farm unions and the Prairie wheat pools began in the early 1920s, and they, too, would be participating in major political battles in the Great Depression.

In the latter half of the decade the agricultural depression lifted temporarily, and there was also an upturn in the urban economy with considerable expansion in the automobile and other mass production industries. But working people did not fare well. Unemployment was seldom below five per cent and was often much higher in the seasonal and unstable resource industries related to forestry, mining and the fisheries. The same was true for those workers involved in urban construction, agricultural labour, and the construction, maintenance and operation of railways and other transportation facilities. Of the advanced industrial economies Canada was one of the most unstable because of its heavy reliance on exporting agricultural and unprocessed resource products. This caused instability not only for agricultural and resource workers but also for those engaged in manufacturing, transportation and the service industries. The Canadian economy was lopsided and precarious even during periods of relative prosperity on the international scene.

The Canada of the 1920s was especially precarious for working people. Trade unions hardly extended beyond the skilled crafts, and even these were on the decline and becoming less effective in the late 1920s. The positive state as we have come to know it since World War II did not yet exist. There was no unemployment insurance and virtually no organized welfare system. There was no hospital coverage or medicare system. Except for a minority there was no such thing as workers' compensation. There was almost no assistance to the disabled or the elderly except for a niggardly old age pension with a means test which was squeezed out of a reluctant government by farmer and worker Members of Parliament in 1926. Family allowances did not exist. State-sponsored homes for the elderly and subsidized low cost housing were almost non-existent. Universities were the preserve of the rich and technical schools were few and far between. Most working people, in fact, could not afford to finish high school, and some entered the work force before finishing elementary school. Such things as maternity leave and affirmative action programmes would have been considered wildly utopian.

In short, the Canadian working family of 1929 lived an incredibly insecure life. An accident or illness in the family could put them in debt for life—and if it happened to be the breadwinner who was hurt or taken ill, the family could be faced with actual hunger in short order. Unemployment was to be dreaded most of all. Periodic layoffs, always common in Canada and especially so in the resource industries, brought severe hardships to tens of thousands of Canadian families even during the most prosperous years. Prolonged periods of widespread unemployment during depressions meant human suffering on a scale which would provoke rioting in the streets today. Most people had nowhere to turn but to relatives or the tender mercies of private charity or, in some cases, to municipal relief which was inadequate and often administered in a humiliating manner.

When the Great Depression struck in the fall of 1929 it very soon affected most of the population. But it was unimaginable catastrophe to the hundreds of thousands who would soon be unemployed. The collection of statistics was an extremely inexact science in the 1930s and government statistics about unemployment generally erred on the side of conservatism. Those statistics admitted that about 13 per cent of the work force were unemployed in 1930, and this figure would soar to about 27 per cent in 1933. During January of that year the unemployment rate is estimated to have exceeded 30 per cent.

Unemployment was not distributed evenly throughout the population. Particular regional, age, ethnic and occupational groups were affected more than others. Those areas dependent upon resource industries, agriculture and construction were hardest hit. Wheat prices hit a 400 year low and the agricultural collapse was compounded by drought. Resource markets disappeared and prices hit rock bottom. The construction industry collapsed, and both domestic and foreign markets for forestry products were lost. The transportation industry was affected by all of these events. The people most immediately and severely hit by unemployment worked in such industries as forestry, mining, agriculture, construction and transportation. Many of these were recent immigrants from the late 1920s. A disproportionate number were also single, under thirty years of age and accustomed to moving frequently from one locality to another in search of jobs. They constituted an indispensable part of the Canadian work force and yet were among the least protected of workers— they performed many of the less desirable jobs at lower than average wages and suffered a relatively high incidence of unemployment even during prosperous years. The Canadian economy could not have existed without them. Perhaps the best description of the role of these people is that provided by Professor H. M. Cassidy, one of the foremost experts on unemployment in Canada during the 1930s.

> Single men, or men detached from their families, were particularly important in serving the needs of Canadian industry. They provided the manpower for logging, mining, railroad construction, railroad maintenance and seasonal work on the farms. Typically they lived while they had jobs in camps in the wilderness and they returned to the main cities when their jobs came to an end. Thus, in the winter months when work was slack and in the years of depression, great numbers of these men congregated in Vancouver, Calgary, Regina, Winnipeg, Montreal, Toronto, Halifax and other centres. In these cities they were pools of labour which could be drawn upon when necessary by the extractive industries.[1]

Most of these people would be driven from locality to locality throughout the 1930s. They had been the single transient workers so crucial to the economy and now they were the single transient unemployed shunned by the local authorities as an unwanted expense and feared by the established order as a potential source of disorder or even revolution. By 1931 these "regular" transients had been joined by thousands more who had been laid off from the secondary industries, young people who had left school because of poverty in the home, and farmers' sons who had fled from rural destitution in search of jobs. Single men were soon joined by married transients and significant numbers of single women who moved from place to place in search of employment.[2]

Federal government officials estimated that by 1932 there were at least 70,000 "single homeless unemployed males" travelling about the country in search of work. Some put the number of single unemployed, including those not classified as "homeless," at double or triple that number.[3] There were no real estimates of the numbers of families and single females who could be classified as "homeless transients."

The most common method of travel from town to town and province to province was by freight train, or "riding the rods." This became almost a way of life for tens of thousands of men and considerable numbers of women and children.

> In the summer months of 1931 and 1932 tens of thousands of men were on the road. Almost every freight train that the transcontinental traveller saw in the summer of 1932 in Northern Ontario and Western Canada had its quota of free passengers, often 50 or 100 or even more. Young boys of 15 and 16 years were among the box car tourists. Girl hoboes were frequently encountered and there were even men with their wives and children.[4]

Riding the freights was illegal under the Railway Act but it became so common that the law was often ignored as unenforceable by the RCMP and provincial police and even by the railway police on trains carrying empty box cars or bulk commodities where there was no danger of theft. Local and provincial authorities sometimes even encouraged the practice as a means of keeping the unemployed moving. In some areas it became common for train crews to cooperate by slowing down or stopping trains at places convenient for people to climb aboard or disembark. There grew up in many towns areas known as "jungles"—makeshift shelters, usually near the main railway lines, where the unemployed would stay a few days while they searched for employment or relief assistance before moving on to the next major centre.

Riding the rods was by no stretch of the imagination a romantic pastime engaged in by aimless youths in search of adventure. It was a hard and dangerous means of travel in which many people were killed and many more maimed or broken in health. Many fell beneath the trains. Some were suffocated when trains went through mountain tunnels and there were instances of men freezing to death during the winter months. Disease probably caused even more deaths than accidents.

By 1932 the number of people riding the rods and the death toll and conditions among them had reached the proportions of a national scandal. Labour organizations, clergymen, opposition politicians and a few newspapers were demanding that something be done. Rev. Andrew Roddan of First United Church in Vancouver worked among the poor and the unemployed. He publicized the plight of the rod riders in *Canada's Untouchables* which was published in 1932.[5] In the same year the Fort William, Ontario, Labour Council sent a message to Prime Minister Bennett requesting an alternative to rod riding because of the number being killed in their vicinity.[6]

An examination of the relief system in Canada at the time will reveal why so many of the unemployed were driven to riding the rods. Relief for the unemployed had always been primarily a municipal responsibility in Canada although the provinces and the federal government provided a proportion of the costs. The relief system of most municipalities in the 1920s and early 1930s was rudimentary, to say the least. They had strict residency requirements even for the married unemployed and many provided no relief whatsoever for single men. Hardly any municipalities provided any form of relief for single transients. This was a conscious policy to discourage the congregation of jobless men from other areas.

This policy did not change substantially during the first two years of the Depression. While the federal government stepped in to provide some public works and some relief assistance to provinces and municipalities there were no specific provisions for the single unemployed under the federal Unemployment Relief Acts of 1930 and 1931. The fact that there was no federal involvement meant that provinces were reluctant to provide assistance for fear they would be inundated by an influx from other provinces. This was especially true for British Columbia where the unemployed from the Prairies would gather during the winter months. It was a "pass the buck" system.

The result was that food and shelter for the single unemployed was largely left to the vagaries of private charitable organizations. The custom in most towns and cities was for churches or charities to provide hostels to supply food and a bed for a few days at most, after which the transients were expected to move on. These institutions were notoriously inadequate during the best years when they were designed only for the hard core "unemployable." They were utterly incapable of handling the thousands of able-bodied men who made up the vast majority of destitute transients throughout the 1930s.

The churches and private charities were soon overwhelmed by the magnitude of the problems. Municipal governments had to become involved, but they could not and in many cases did not want to handle the situation adequately. Many towns and cities merely let men sleep in the police stations and often on bare floors with no bedding other than what they might supply themselves. A typical policy was to allow an unemployed transient to spend one night in the police station and then leave town the next day or face arrest for vagrancy.

In cases where cities did provide municipal hostels they were usually "rough and ready" as revealed by a survey of hostels in Ontario during the winter of 1930-31.

> The hostel accommodation provided was usually rough and ready. In one city, for instance, a large room above a garage was fitted up with beds made from two-by-four lumber and chicken wire netting. In another, an old jail was used which had to be fumigated and cleaned before the first batch of boarders entered the building. In some instances the hostel accommodation was criticized not only by the men themselves but also by outsiders because of the absence of proper sanitary facilities and the presence of vermin and filth. [7]

Soup kitchens were run either by private charity or city governments. Rarely were more than two meals a day provided, and often there was only one. Further, the term "meal" could be considered an exaggeration. Ronald Liversedge, who had the misfortune of spending part of a winter unemployed in Sudbury, Ontario, describes one such soup kitchen in his *Recollections of the On-to-Ottawa Trek, 1935:*

> The process of obtaining a meal at the soup kitchen was truly an ordeal. The long line-up of hundreds of men in sub-zero weather, slowly, very slowly, moving ahead, a few steps, and then a wait. Sometimes it took an hour to reach the house in the middle of a short row of dwelling houses (near the CPR station) where the beans were boiling in the water.
>
> To me the line-up was worse on days when there had been a rise in temperature and a slight thaw, then one shuffled slowly ahead through a foot and a half of frozen slush. In the case of

myself and many others shod only in broken-down oxford shoes, it was a very unpleasant experience.

Arriving at the house, one entered the small room just large enough to hold the stove with the two big pots, a short counter and room in front of the counter for the boys to file past. After receiving the food, the boys proceeded to the top of the stairway which led to the basement and our dining room.

On reaching the dining room, I at once realized the reason for the slowness of the whole procedure. In this dimly lit small basement there were three short trestle and plank tables around which the men stood to eat. Each man coming down from the kitchen had to wait on the stairs with his rapidly-cooling plate of beans, for a stand-in at this veritable feast of the passover.

The atmosphere in the basement was like that in a chilly, moldy crypt. The tables were covered with ice, and beans, and pieces of wet bread. The floor was ankle deep in churned up sludge, and at the out door into the alley at the back, there was always a "spic-and-span" young "Mountie" on guard to see that nobody threw the valuable food into the garbage can.[8]

The soup kitchen described by Liversedge must surely have been among the worst in the country. But complaints from across Canada indicated that conditions in many others were only slightly better.

The fact that in many towns the unemployed could obtain shelter and food for only one day or a few days at most meant that they had no choice but to ride the rods however uninviting the prospect.

Finding that their welcome in a new community would soon wear out, many of the transients moved from place to place, even during the middle of winter, picking up a nights lodging and a few meals in one centre and then travelling by freight train to the nearest city where they would repeat the performance.[9]

It was like being battered from "pillar to post." The time and effort required for mere survival left little time to search for employment even in those rare instances where temporary jobs might be available. To make matters worse, the government of Ontario, believing the predictions of business leaders that a great upturn in the economy was underway, closed most publicly supported hostels and soup kitchens in the spring of 1931. Thousands were faced with a threat to their very survival. "Since the employment situation did not improve very much and since private relief measures were inadequate large numbers of men were compelled to sleep out of doors during the summer and to obtain food by begging."[10]

THE UNEMPLOYED ORGANIZE AND FIGHT

Before the 1930s the unemployed had never been organized except in isolated local situations and for very short periods. Unemployed people have always been difficult to organize because, unlike working people, they have no labour power to withdraw, nor do they have the financial means to sustain an elaborate organization. Organizing the jobless thus appears to be futile. It was especially difficult to organize the single unemployed in Canada because they were constantly on the move, making it hard to develop or sustain any form of stable leadership. Further, most unemployed people were too busy looking for jobs or merely holding body and soul together to devote time and attention to organization.

There were also psychological factors at play. The jobless were isolated from their comrades. And in our society, where everyone is expected to work and where people are judged by their work, there has always been a "blame the victim" syndrome. The supporters of the *status quo* and the opinion leaders had, up to 1930, usually been successful in selling the idea that unemployed people were lazy or misfits. It was so much a part of the capitalist ethic and the popular wisdom that many—and perhaps most—unemployed people at least partially believed it themselves. To be out of work in such a society sapped people's self-confidence and sometimes destroyed their pride. They tended to blame themselves rather than the system.

The onslaught of the Great Depression changed all of this for both the married and the single unemployed. The myths about "misfits" and "lack of initiative" could no longer be sustained with 30 per cent of the work force without jobs. The humiliating means tests for "gunny sack" relief enraged unemployed working-class families.[11] And the single unemployed, now in the tens of thousands, were not about to put up with the filthy hostels and degrading soup kitchens and high-handed authority which had for so long been the lot of smaller numbers of unemployed. These people were used to relatively steady employment and the status which went with it. Authorities who treated them like "bums" or "hoboes" were due for a rude awakening.

The unemployed were not about to accept their condition without protest. But at the beginning of the Depression they were not yet organized and there were few existing organizations or political formations interested in organizing or agitating on their behalf. The mainstream trade union federations of the day consisted of the Trades and Labour Congress (TLC) and the All-Canadian Congress of Labour (ACCL) nationally and the Canadian Catholic Congress of Labour (CCCL) which was limited to Quebec. The TLC, the largest union federation, was composed exclusively of international craft unions with a conservative craft union approach to organizing. They did not believe in organizing unskilled workers, let alone the unemployed. The ACCL was not so narrow in its outlook but showed no interest in organizing the unemployed. And in this period the CCCL was even more conservative than the craft unionists in the TLC.

The leaders of all three mainstream trade union federations had no effective strategy for defending the interests of their own members in the face of the Depression. They had a difficult enough time holding their own organizations together without worrying about the plight of the unemployed. Most could offer little more than sympathy.

The only trade union group willing to try organizing the un-employed was the Workers' Unity League (WUL), which had been organized by supporters of the Communist Party of Canada in the 1930s as a rival to the more orthodox trade union federations. They concentrated on organizing among immigrants, resource workers and unskilled labourers who had previously been left out of the mainstream trade union movement in Canada. The WUL regarded the unemployed as a potential organizational and political base well worth cultivating. In stepping into this vacuum the radical activists of the WUL were able and willing to employ the militant tactics necessitated by the task at hand.

The first known organization of unemployed was the Vancouver Unemployed Workers' Association which was formed in September 1929. [12] By 1931 there were unemployed associations in nearly every city and major town in the country. In the autumn of 1931 there were six such organizations in Saskatoon alone and most cities of any size could boast more than one. [13] There were often separate organizations for married unemployed, single unemployed, un-employed war veterans and the wives and families of unemployed. There were also supporting organizations of employed people.

While many of the unemployed associations grew up almost spontaneously and quite independent of one another they soon began to develop regional, provincial and national coordination. This is where the Workers' Unity League performed an indispensable role. They were able to coordinate the activities of the individual groups and eventually to make the unemployed movement national in scope and give it clear and consistent objectives. What began as sporadic protest evolved into a national political movement with a specific, positive and realistic programme. They demanded work and wages as quickly as possible and in the meantime public relief under dignified conditions.

The organized unemployed were soon able to exert considerable pressure upon politicians and relief administrations, particularly at the local level. Since they had no pipelines to the corridors of power and could not apply conventional trade union tactics like collective bargaining, they had to be extremely imaginative in their actions. They adopted a wide variety of tactics: mass meetings, petitions and delegations to the three levels of government, demonstrations, sit-ins at relief offices, picket lines and strikes on relief projects. [14] Emphasis was also placed on developing alliances with trade unions, farm organizations, sympathetic church activists, and women's organizations.

By the spring of 1931 it was evident that the movement had become national in scope. A large demonstration of unemployed on Parliament Hill on March 15 sparked much comment throughout the nation. [15] The WUL also carried out a well coordinated action on April 15 involving simultaneous demonstrations in Montreal, Ottawa, Sudbury, Winnipeg, where there were clashes between demonstrators and police, and other cities. [16] On May 1 there were May Day demonstrations across the country with demonstrations being broken up by police in Port Arthur and Calgary and significant clashes in several other cities. [17] Most of these actions involved both single and married unemployed and many were supported by local trade unions. During 1931 there were also at least seven major strikes by men employed on "make work" relief projects and several instances of "cessation" of work by men working for "direct relief" in kind as opposed to monetary payment. [18] All of these events coincided with bitter trade union struggles of which the best known is the Estevan-Bienfait coal miners' strike in the early autumn.

The organized unemployed and their allies were insisting on being heard and demanding that all levels of government do something about the national scandal of unemployment. The battle had been engaged but it had barely begun.

Footnotes

1. H.M. Cassidy, "Relief and Other Social Services for Transients," in L. Richter (ed.) *Canada's Unemployment Problem* (Toronto: Macmillan, 1939), p. 175.
   Dr. H.M. Cassidy was perhaps the most informed person in Canada on the problems associated with unemployment and relief during the 1930s.

In 1932 Cassidy was Assistant Professor of Social Science at the University of Toronto and served as Secretary and Director of Research of The Unemployment Research Committee of Ontario, under whose auspices he published a book and several articles on unemployment. Cassidy later served for a time as Director of Social Welfare for the Province of British Columbia before accepting an appointment as Professor of Economics at the University of California in Berkeley.

2. *Ibid.*, p. 177.
3. H.M. Cassidy, *Unemployment and Relief in Ontario 1929-1932* (Toronto and Vancouver: J.M. Dent and Sons, Ltd., 1932), p. 165.
4. Cassidy in Richter (ed.), *op. cit.*, p. 176.
5. Rev. Andrew Roddan, *Canada's Untouchables* (Vancouver: The Clarke and Stuart Company Ltd., 1932).
6. Public Archives of Canada (PAC) *Bennett Papers*, 1932.
7. Cassidy, *op. cit.*, p. 204.
8. Ronald Liversedge, *Recollections of the On-to-Ottawa Trek*, edited by Victor Hoar (Toronto: McClelland and Stewart Ltd., 1973), pp. 9-10.
9. Cassidy, *op. cit.*, p. 206.
10. *Ibid.*, p. 207.
11. In many cities, Vancouver being an example, unemployed families in need of relief did not receive a cash payment. The head of the family had to line up on relief day and receive groceries which were carried home in a gunny sack. It was intended to be humiliating since all the neighbours would know who was on relief and it was assumed that unemployed people could not be trusted to handle money properly. By the end of the 1930s this outrage had ended in most cities after tremendous protests by the organized unemployed and their supporters.
12. Stuart Jamieson, *Times of Trouble: Labour Unrest and Industrial Conflict in Canada, 1900-1966*, Study No. 22, Task Force on Labour Relations, 1966-1968, Information Canada, 1971, p. 221.
13. Lorne Brown, "Unemployment Relief Camps in Saskatchewan, 1933-1936," *Saskatchewan History*, Vol. XXIII, No. 3, p. 84.
14. *Ibid.*, also Hoar, *op. cit.*
15. Ottawa *Morning Citizen*, March 15, 1931.
16. *Canadian Annual Review (CAR)*, 1930-31, p. 454.
17. *Ibid.*
18. *CAR*, 1932, p. 417.

Demonstration in support of the unemployed, Victoria, April 1935.
(Photo #D-6602, Provincial Archives of B.C.)

CHAPTER II
Promises Unfulfilled

In order to understand the attitude of the Bennett government towards the organized unemployed, and particularly the single unemployed, one must examine the attitude prevalent among mainstream political and business leaders during the early 1930s.

The so-called Great Crash and the beginning of heavy unemployment occurred in the autumn of 1929. MacKenzie King's Liberal government in Ottawa refused to recognize the magnitude of the disaster and contended that unemployment was not a serious problem. R.B. Bennett made the Depression an issue in the election of 1930 and promised to end unemployment. The Conservative strategy for ending unemployment emphasized their traditional policy of high protective tariffs. The idea was to protect Canadian industry in the domestic market and to use high tariffs against foreign products as a bargaining tool to obtain bilateral trade agreements with other countries. Bennett claimed that Canada could use Conservative tariff strategy to "blast our way into the markets of the world." As a stop gap measure the Conservatives also promised major public works projects to put people to work immediately while the trade strategy was taking effect.

The Bennett government was elected in the fall of 1930 on their programme to fight the Depression. The tariff policy was a total failure. The drought and the low prices for agricultural and resource products destroyed the domestic market, tariffs or no tariffs. Other industrialized countries were also busy "blasting" their way into the markets of the world, but most had bigger economic "guns" than Canada.

The federal government did undertake several public works projects and provided more relief money to the provinces, but the amount turned out to be pitifully inadequate. Both government and business leaders had underestimated the magnitude of the Depression. Even when the extent of it dawned upon them, they hoped, argued and predicted that it was temporary. As late as 1932 the leaders of Canadian chartered banks were insisting "prosperity is just around the corner."

In the meantime, sacrifices were deemed necessary—and these sacrifices were unevenly distributed. The federal government adopted a strategy of limiting public expenditures, and especially public borrowing, so as not to compete with the private sector. Working people, and particularly the unemployed, would have to suffer while the private sector recovered. Governments were forced to undergo some increased spending to avoid widespread starvation and total chaos, but they did so with great reluctance. They utterly refused to undertake the type of massive government spending on public works programmes which might have made a serious dent in the level of unemployment.

The need to please the business community in order to maintain the credit rating of the country was cited repeatedly by Prime Minister Bennett as a reason for not embarking upon more ambitious public works programmes. This is borne out in a letter to Conservative M.P. R.B. Hanson on October 22, 1931: "To maintain our credit, we must practice the most rigid economy and not needlessly spend a single cent."[1]

Conservative spokesmen maintained this stance throughout their term of office and even after the introduction of the Bennett New Deal in 1935. By 1935 they were finally willing to attempt to regulate the economy but not yet to attempt a Keynesian solution on a meaningful scale. George Perley, Minister of Defence, repeated the same arguments in the spring of 1935 when he admitted that the government was being besieged by numerous "responsible citizens" to undertake a serious "work and wages" programme but claimed that such a policy would be economic folly.

> It might result in compromising the orderly revival of industry, which at present is progressing hopefully. Every undue burden of this character which is assumed lessens the rate at which recovery will take place.[2]

This attitude, maintained by the federal government over a five-year period, met with the approval of most of the business community, much of the press and the main leaders of the Liberal Opposition. The Liberals roundly criticized the Bennett government for the ravages of the Depression but refused to depart from the old economic orthodoxy themselves. That orthodoxy viewed the running of a government much like the running of a private business. Deficit financing was frowned upon, and it was considered almost as important for a government to have a balanced budget as for a corporation to show a profit. On economic matters the main differences between Liberals and Conservatives revolved around trade policies. The Liberals generally favoured freer trade and the Conservatives higher protective tariffs. It would not be until after World War II that some degree of "Keynesianism" would be accepted by all major parties in Canada.

While governments were busy attempting to make ends meet, and in the case of some of the poorer provinces trying to avoid bankruptcy, private business and industry continued to lay off thousands of workers and to impose major wage cuts on those still employed. Some industries rolled back wages annually for five successive years and put thousands more on part-time employment.

Both working people and farmers were taking a terrible battering and unrest quickly grew to the point where significant sectors of the population were in a very combative mood. Neither the mainstream political parties nor the mainstream trade unions could answer the needs of the time, and many people turned to new economic and political formations. Left-wing farmers and intellectuals joined with the Independent Labour Party (ILP) of J.S. Woodsworth to found the Co-operative Commonwealth Federation (CCF) in 1932 as a farmer-labour social democratic alternative to the Liberals and Conservatives. In the years to follow came populist protest parties like Social Credit in Alberta and the Union Nationale in Quebec both at first a mixture of left and right ideas, though they would soon veer far to the right.

Some of the more radical working people would join the Communist Party of Canada which had existed since 1922 but which underwent rapid growth after 1930. Thousands more would flock to the banner of the Workers' Unity League (WUL) which had been founded by communists as a radical union federation in 1930. The WUL organized in areas and occupations which had barely been touched by previous union federations. They were especially active in the mining and forestry industries, whose workers were among the hardest hit by the Depression. It was here that layoffs and wage rollbacks reached epidemic proportions and threatened to destroy entire communities. Bitter strikes were fought in most of the coal fields and many of the hard rock mining towns of Canada during the first three years of the Depression. Most of these were strikes of the "desperation variety" in that they were merely attempts to prevent wage rollbacks or achieve or maintain union recognition.

Most of the strikes between 1930 and 1934 were led by the WUL, the only union federation putting up serious resistance to the rollbacks—and this very fact drew thousands more to their banner. The WUL also organized the unemployed for the first time in history. Concerted action between militant trade unions and the organized unemployed made for a volatile mixture: the unemployed, by the very nature of their struggle, had to go beyond conventional trade union tactics; the trade unions had to go further as well if they were to have any hope of success in the economic circumstances and the political climate then prevailing. Both groups *had* to be disruptive and threatening if they were to gain any concessions from either governments or private employers. Their very livelihood was at stake.

The results were predictable in that street demonstrations became commonplace and often resulted in clashes with the police which turned into riots. There were disturbances in soup kitchens and hostels. Communists and other radicals were beginning to attract large crowds to their rallies. Left-wing literature was more popular than ever. A movement for radical social change was gaining momentum as the Depression worsened.

The federal government and constituted authority in general found themselves caught on the horns of a dilemma at least partly of their own making. Because of their obsession with the country's credit rating, their aversion to competing in the money markets with private industry, and their desire to provide a favourable business climate generally, they were unable to take measures to significantly alleviate the suffering of the population. Hence they provided direct stimulants to the economy and assistance to the unemployed only to the extent absolutely necessary to prevent a general breakdown in law and order. But working people could not be expected to suffer in silence and their unrest continued to increase—and this in turn did nothing to enhance the credit rating and the general business climate. By the very nature of their approach to the situation the federal government and the established order set the stage for the greatest period of political turmoil and the greatest curtailment of civil liberties in the peacetime history of Canada up to that time.

Political leaders at all three levels of government, the press, the judiciary, and relief and police officials prepared the ground for political repression by launching tremendous propaganda campaigns to discredit militant trade unions, the organized unemployed, radical political parties and political dissent in general. They whipped up a general hysteria about the threat of communism and bloody revolution which would threaten people's lives and property. In the early years of the Depression these forces probably represented majority opinion and many politicians genuinely believed in the "communist threat."

The prime minister led the way by boasting that he would apply "the iron heel of ruthlessness" to combating communism and any similar doctrine. Bennett tended to portray organizers and leaders of the unemployed as malcontents or radicals with ulterior motives. "Whenever the minds of people are disturbed by economic conditions, there are always agitators who capitalize and exploit 'humanitarianism' and the sympathy that is latent in all of us for the underdog."[3] It followed that the existing order must be defended with increased vigour; yielding to the demands of agitators and making concessions to organized opposition groups must be resisted at all costs.

Initially most of the country's daily newspapers were fully in support of Bennett's attitude, though many of them would eventually alter their opinions in the coming years as the organized unemployed began to receive broad public support. Editorialists opined that most of the unemployed would be grateful for government efforts and accept their hardships if it were not for radical troublemakers agitating among an otherwise contented and law-abiding population. It followed from this line of reasoning that people would continue to support the established order if only the government cracked down on agitators and prevented them from poisoning people's minds with radical doctrines. The Montreal *Gazette* expressed this point of view in an editorial supporting the arrest and prosecution of prominent communists in August 1931.

> Extraordinary efforts are being made by governments to provide for the natural needs of people who are in distress through unemployment. What happens to a man's mind in times of depression is just as important as what happens to his body, and therefore it is incumbent upon the authorities to safeguard the individual mind from corruption when it is threatened by the spread of the revolutionary doctrine it is known the Communists are preaching vocally and spreading by propaganda, and with an aggressiveness that has become bolder and more intense in a belief that the economic situation today affords them better opportunity to prosecute their nefarious work.[4]

Prominent police and judicial figures joined the chorus calling for a crackdown on dissenters. A common argument was to portray communism and socialism as foreign doctrines and almost any kind of militant protest or radical dissent as un-Canadian or against the British system of constitutional government. This fit in with a general suspicion of foreigners and prejudice against non-British immigrants prevalent in Canada at the time and it could be used to divide working people among themselves if thousands of native-born Canadians could be encouraged to blame their plight on immigrants competing in the job markets.

Toronto police chief D.C. Draper and Judge Emerson Coatsworth, Chairman of the Toronto Board of Police Commissioners, were well known for their war on agitation and their distrust of immigrants in what was one of the more repressive cities in Canada. Sir William Mulock, Chief Justice of Ontario and Chancellor of the University of Toronto, was notorious for his hatred of left-wing radicalism which he claimed came from agitation by foreigners. To Mulock, who was respected by the press as an "elder statesman," having served many years in Laurier's cabinet before World War I and later been appointed Chief Justice, communist doctrine was like a communicable disease brought into the country by foreigners and which could easily be prevented with more vigilance by the authorities. In February 1931 Mulock expressed such sentiments in a speech before a banquet sponsored by the Canadian National Exhibition for 1000 stock-breeders and exhibitors at the Royal York Hotel. He urged all those who valued "British freedom" to unite behind a campaign to ban communists from Canada and to stamp out "the treasonable and insidious virus with which wicked men would inoculate the Canadian body politic."[5] Sir William then provided a description of what was in store for Canada if the communist "virus" was not stamped out.

> If Canada is content to have her laws made by those who deny the existence of God, who would suppress religion, who would destroy the sacredness of marriage and who would nationalize women, who would extinguish the love of parents for their children or children for their parents, who would abolish homelife—one of the chief sources of human happiness; who would deprive children in their tender years of a mother's care and expose them to the imminent danger of growing up as criminals; who would rob all citizens by any degree of force, up to that of murder, of all their worldly goods and leave them penniless; who would make it a crime for one to save; would deprive people of liberty and make slaves of them to the State.
>
> If, I say, these are the conditions which Canada is content to have established in Canada then let her open her doors wide and admit into full citizenship the millions of people of that class.

But if Canada does not wish to become a hell on earth she should rid herself at once of those who would, if they could, make her such, and let her prevent any of that kind of people ever setting foot on Canadian soil.[6]

Sir William's speech—strange, to say the least, for a prominent member of the politically "neutral" judiciary—was vigorously applauded by the crowd and the head table guests, among whom were included Honourable Leopold Macaulay, Provincial Secretary of Ontario; Honourable Gideon Robertson, Federal Minister of Labour; Judge Emerson Coatsworth, Chairman of the Toronto Board of Police Commissioners; Police Chief D.C. Draper; and Canon H.J. Cody, Chairman of the Board of Governors of the University of Toronto. Macaulay and Robertson made brief statements declaring their full agreement with Mulock's sentiments though Robertson also took the occasion to reassure the public that the federal government had matters under control and that the "blood-thirsty" communists were not yet a serious threat to the state.

The Mulock speech was also well received in the press. Three of the four Toronto dailies congratulated him for warning the public of the imminent danger. The *Mail and Empire* emphasized Sir William's non-partisanship and pointed out that, being Chief Justice of Ontario and chancellor of the University of Toronto,

he may be regarded as having passed beyond the realm of ordinary combative politics. It must be conceded that, as an elder statesman who has given a lifetime of service to the state he has nothing but the welfare of that state in mind.[7]

Canadian economic and political ruling circles were obviously worried about working-class unrest. Why else would leading newspapers and politicians applaud the ludicrous and outlandish statements of Sir William Mulock? During normal times such statements by so prominent an individual would probably have been ignored out of embarrassment. And these types of attacks were not limited to Toronto but were repeated in different variations, though usually in less extreme language, throughout the country by editorialists, politicians and civic and judicial officials. They appear to have been part of a concerted effort to make political protest appear illegitimate and to justify repressive measures against radical dissenters.

By 1931 matters had long since gone beyond mere verbal attack and repressive measures were being undertaken by all three levels of government. Government officials already possessed various powers which could be used to intimidate and neutralize dissenters and the use of these powers escalated in the latter part of 1930 and throughout 1931.

Significant numbers of the unemployed, and particularly the single unemployed, were immigrants because immigrants had been concentrated in the resource industries and other occupations hardest hit by the Depression. The authorities had more legal power over immigrants than over native-born Canadians: under Canadian immigration laws immigrants who had lived in Canada for less than five years could be deported for becoming "a public charge"—for being on any form of public assistance. The law stated that they were liable for deportation but not that they would necessarily be deported, which placed important discretionary power in the hands of the authorities. Relief officials could intimidate immigrants who were inclined to be too vocal in standing up for their rights.

The widespread prejudice against immigrants, particularly those from Central and Eastern Europe, and the desire of local government to reduce relief costs, led to large-scale victimization of unemployed immigrants. The most common method of deporting people in this category was for the local authorities to request the federal government to take action in individual cases and then the immigration officials would begin deportation proceedings. This power was frequently used by local officials not only to intimidate those on relief but also to discourage immigrants from even applying for relief. Many a family went hungry rather than risk deportation.

Harry Cassidy, in his 1932 study of unemployment relief in Ontario, cites many instances of intimidation and complains about municipal officials having so much power over people's lives. "This is a dangerous power in the hands of the local authorities in a period of crisis when panicky action is all too easily taken."[8] That this power was frequently abused is evident from government deportation statistics. During the fiscal year ending March 31, 1932, there were 7024 deportations from Canada, including 4507 described as "having been public charges."[9] For the fiscal year ending March 31, 1933, there were 7131, including 4916 for being in need of relief.[10] Some of these deportations were technically voluntary, particularly in the case of immigrants from Britain, who had become disillusioned with Canada and agreed to be deported in the hope that they would have a better chance of work or assistance from the government or their relatives back home. Government statistics did not distinguish between "voluntary" and involuntary deportations but from newspaper accounts and debates in the House of Commons it appears that the majority were involuntary.

36

Immigrants who had been in Canada longer than five years, even those who had become Canadian citizens, were not safe from the power of the immigration authorities. The Immigration Act also provided that anyone not born in Canada, even if a naturalized citizen, could be deported for advocating overthrow by force of constituted authority "or by word or act creat[ing] or attempt[ing] to create riot or public disorder in Canada."[11]

The methods used to deport people for both political and ordinary criminal offences short-circuited trial by jury and the normal legal process. A person scheduled for deportation could be represented by a lawyer but was not given a hearing in open court. The case could be appealed to an internal committee of the Department of Immigration but this hearing as well was held in camera. People could be, and sometimes were, arrested by the RCMP in the middle of the night and sent by train to Halifax where they were imprisoned in the immigration sheds pending disposal of each case by the Department of Immigration.[12] Thousands of miles from relatives and friends, they would be greatly handicapped in obtaining the services of lawyers and other assistance. One example cited by J.S. Woodsworth in the House of Commons involved three men, Daniel Holmer (Chomiski), Orton Wade, and Konrad Cassinger, who were seized by the RCMP in Winnipeg and transported to Halifax to await deportation. Although the three were known radicals, they had no police records, and one had been in Canada for twenty years and had a Canadian-born wife and child.

The case of the three Winnipeg men was by no means atypical. The government did not keep statistics on people deported for political as opposed to ordinary criminal offences, and, at any rate, police often arrested people when they broke up political demonstrations and then charged them with ordinary criminal offences, such as assault, property damage, and disturbing the peace. Those who fell into the political category, however, would be in the hundreds.[13] Many were deported to European countries governed by fascist or military regimes where communists and socialists and other labour radicals could be imprisoned or even executed upon arrival. The *Canadian Forum* documented a number of these cases.

There were 14,154 deportations in the period April 1, 1931, to March 31, 1933, up from fewer than 25,000 deportations to all countries in the entire thirty years before 1930.[14] The immigration laws were obviously being grossly abused both to save the government money and to attack their political critics. And many officials were pressing the federal government to take an even harder approach. In 1932 Commissioner MacBrien of the RCMP suggested publicly that *all* communist immigrants be deported, presumably on the grounds of their political allegiance alone. [15]

Those dissidents who were not immigrants, and this would include most, could be harassed in a variety of ways and under a great variety of laws. Communists, left-wing labour organizations and the organized unemployed were harassed on a fairly continual basis by the RCMP and special squads of city police from the summer of 1930, even before the Bennett government was elected to office. Much of this harassment was carried out under the direction of provincial and local authorities but usually with the active encouragement of the federal government and the RCMP themselves.

During 1930, Communist Party offices were raided and their literature and files seized in Montreal, Winnipeg, and Vancouver. [16] There was also a raid in Port Arthur on the offices of the Canadian Labour Defence League (CLDL), a communist led organization specializing in defending people charged with political offences. [17] That same year parades and demonstrations of the unemployed were broken up by police across the country resulting in large numbers of injuries and arrests. [18] This type of activity escalated during 1931 as the unemployed became angrier and better organized.

One of the favourite tactics employed in Toronto was for the Board of Police Commissioners to deny the use of public halls to organizations they deemed to be radical or subversive. Such organizations had to meet in public parks or on street corners. These meetings were then dispersed by the police, often in a violent manner, on the grounds that they were a threat to public order. One such event involving a mass rally at Queen's Park was described in the Toronto *Telegram*.

> Inspector Marshall, with his force of men, was pressing the crowd outwards towards the parliament buildings while another line of police—pressing northward caught the crowds between them.... The motorcyles... roared their way making large gaps and laneways in the crowd... Older men, unable to move as fast, were trampled down by the crowds, including the police. Women ran for the shelter of the streets and were chased. Police boots are said to have assisted fists and sticks. Elbows, too, were used to break up the crowds. How the mounted men were able to prevent their horses from trampling people under is still a miracle. [19]

Most major cities witnessed similar events on a fairly regular basis. Stuart Jamieson describes the situation in Vancouver, one of the most volatile centres.

The married unemployed were given relief by means of a "gunny sack parade" at which married men lined up in front of an old church building on the Cambie Street grounds to receive their quota of food and tokens exchangeable for shelter and fuel. Mass meetings on the grounds, parades, and protest marches to City Hall by the unemployed, were attacked repeatedly by forces from the RCMP, the provincial police, and a specially trained "riot squad" of mounted city police armed with long, lead-weighted clubs. There were numerous serious riots in which hundreds were injured in Vancouver during the first few years of the Great Depression. [20]

It is likely that a clear majority of riots and major disturbances during the 1930s were provoked by police actions, and some could even be categorized as "police riots" though usually more than the police were rioting by the time they were over. A riot was usually started when police attempted to disperse what was a peaceful though perhaps militant and noisy demonstration or meeting.

One reason for such inappropriate police action could be paranoia on the part of police and other officials. But there were advantages to combating the organized unemployed and radicalism in general. The occasional riot or disturbance was often followed by large-scale arrests. Participants could be charged with assaulting the police, damaging property, creating a public nuisance, disorderly conduct, or a number of other offences. Fines and jail sentences and, in the case of immigrants, deportation would be facing the individuals involved, not only serving as an example but also tying up the protest movement with collecting money for bail, hiring lawyers and dealing with the courts. The very fact that meetings and demonstrations were dispersed by the police and many of the participants arrested could be used to discredit such activities. Loyal citizens were supposed to stoically accept their lot pending the recovery of the economy.

Government officials did not rely solely upon the police and the courts to combat disaffection and dissidence among the population. Right-wing "citizens committees" and vigilante groups were not unknown on the Canadian political scene. Such committees had been formed to work with state officials in defending the *status quo* during the Winnipeg General Strike of 1919. And students of Saskatchewan history will remember that the Ku Klux Klan helped elect the Anderson government in that province in 1929. Such groups mushroomed during the 1930s as they usually do during times of economic and political crisis.

The provincial and federal governments collaborated with right-wing propaganda and vigilante groups throughout the 1930s. They gave them private and sometimes public encouragement. Commissioner MacBrien of the RCMP publicly urged citizens to form such organizations to supplement the work of the police.[21] Colonel Ralph Webb, Mayor of Winnipeg, corresponded with Prime Minister Bennett on the desirability of establishing citizens' committees to combat "subversives" and support the established order.[22] He received encouragement from Bennett.

General A.G.L. McNaughton, Chief of the General Staff, and several of his military officers held private consultations with businessmen to coordinate government and private corporate strategy in combating labour militancy. One such meeting at National Defence Headquarters involved General McNaughton and Major G.R. Turner with J.O. Apps, General Executive Assistant of the CPR, and C.A. Cottrell, Assistant General Manager of the B.C. District of the CPR.[23] They discussed coordinating of the activities of employers and government officials in frustrating a strike of longshoremen and combating radical trade unionists in general on the West Coast. Among the topics discussed was the formation of a "Five Hundred Club" of Vancouver businessmen "along the lines of similar citizens' vigilance committees in cities along the Pacific Coast of the U.S.A." whose purpose would be "to finance an intensive campaign to educate and inform the citizens generally of the true state of affairs and the danger from the radical control of the labour unions."[24]

McNaughton's discussions with the CPR officials says something about the supposed neutrality of the state. But at least the activities being discussed were not illegal and McNaughton even declined a suggestion by Cottrell that government relief funds be used to finance the Five Hundred Club.[25] Prime Minister Bennett, a vocal proponent of law and order in public, was not always so squeamish in his private consultations as revealed by his correspondence with Alex Lockwood, President of the Anti-Communist League of Flin Flon, Manitoba. Lockwood wrote to Bennett to congratulate him for standing up to the communists and to describe the activities and purposes of his organization. "The Anti-Communist League of Flin Flon is a non-political, non-sectarian organization. It stands for the ruthless suppression of Communism in all its forms."[26] Lockwood described the League's activities as being directed towards ridding Flin Flon of "undesirable elements," most of whom were "foreigners" and communists. League members planned to organize throughout the country and were willing to fight what they viewed as communism by both legal and illegal means.

> Should our activities bring us into contact with the law, we still shall not hesitate as we deem Canada to be in dire peril at the present moment and no sacrifice any of us may make will be considered too great a price, if it in turn preserves our Country from the Red Menace.[27]

Lockwood goes on to demand more vigorous action by the authorities against unnamed individuals whom he described as "foreigners" responsible for communistic agitation in the Flin Flon Area.

One would expect the prime minister to ignore Lockwood as an unhealthy fanatic or even instruct the appropriate officials to warn him about staying within the limits of the law. But Bennett's reaction was not only to offer government cooperation but to encourage Lockwood's efforts.

> You should communicate with the Attorney-General of Manitoba, as under our Constitution, matters of this kind come under his jurisdiction. However, if you will send me in confidence the names of those to whom you refer I will ascertain whether or not it is possible to deport them as undesirables.[28]

The prime minister's letter ends with a generous compliment to Lockwood, "Congratulating you upon your fine sense of public duty as a citizen of Canada."[29]

Bennett was also not above making common cause with people who were more explicitly fascist in their politics. In the 1930 election campaign Adrien Arcand of the fascistic Order Patriotique des Goglus received $18,000 from the Conservative Party in return for journalistic support of the Tory cause in Quebec. The arrangement was made after Arcand and a colleague met with Bennett and outlined their "plan of procedures and propaganda."[30] The support of Arcand and his newspapers and movement is credited with helping win twenty-four seats for the Conservatives in Quebec.[31]

In 1934 Adrien Arcand founded Le Parti National Social Chrétien (National Social Christian Party) with himself as leader. The new party patterned itself after German Nazism and Italian fascism.[32] A year later this party would support the Conservatives in the federal election of 1935. Arcand was appointed publicity director for Bennett's campaign in Quebec.[33]

For the purposes of political repression the most sweeping legal powers in the hands of government officials were contained in Section 98 of the Criminal Code. Section 98, which was originally passed in 1919 at the time of the Winnipeg General Strike, made it a crime, punishable by up to twenty years in prison, to belong to any association whose purpose was to bring about governmental, industrial or economic change by force or which advocated the use of force for such purposes. Property belonging, or suspected to belong, to such an association might be seized without warrant and forfeited to the Crown. If it could be shown that a person had attended meetings of such an association, spoken publicly in its support or distributed its literature, "it shall be presumed, in the absence of proof to the contrary, that he is a member of such unlawful association."[34] What was so sweeping about Section 98 was guilt by association, the onus of proof being on the individual and not on the Crown, and the fact that people did not have to be charged with specific actions or conspiracies but could be prosecuted for their beliefs.

On August 11, 1931, Tim Buck and seven other prominent communist leaders were arrested under the instructions of Attorney-General W.H. Price of Ontario. This action was accompanied by raids and seizure of records at the headquarters of the Communist Party and the homes of several prominent communists. Tim Buck and his colleagues were convicted and sentenced to Kingston Penitentiary under Section 98 on the grounds that they belonged to an organization whose purpose was to overthrow by force the prevailing economic and political system.

The communist leaders were not charged with any specific conspiracy to overthrow constituted authority in Canada.[35] The reasoning of the prosecution was that, since the Communist Party of Canada was part of the Communist International and the stated purpose of the International was to promote revolution throughout the world, therefore members of the Communist Party were guilty of violating Section 98.[36] Buck and his colleagues were convicted before Mr. Justice Wright in Toronto and appealed to the Court of Appeal of Ontario, which upheld the verdict. The Appeal Court judgement was delivered by none other than Chief Justice William Mulock who obviously should have been disqualified because of his well known political prejudices.

The temper of the times was such that the authorities felt no embarrassment about such a blatant assault on civil liberties. Those responsible boasted about having carried off a great coup and were anxious to claim credit for a bold stroke against the alleged communist menace. Attorney-General Price had two booklets published alerting the public to the threat of communism and calling for continuing vigilance.[37] One was entitled *Agents of Revolution: A History of the Workers' Unity League, Setting Forth Its Origins and Aims.* This dealt with communist efforts to organize trade unions and warned of the dire consequences to the country should such unions be allowed to exist. The appendix included copies of several letters seized at the home of Tim Buck. The other, *The King vs Buck and Others: The Judgment of the Court of Appeal of Ontario Concerning the Communist Party in Canada,* included the judgement delivered by Sir William Mulock and an introduction by Price in which he explained the need for Section 98 of the Criminal Code.

Though the prosecution of the communists was carried out by the Ontario government because it fell under their jurisdiction, there was undoubtedly close collaboration with the federal authorities. Attorney-General Price stated that the problem of how to control the communists had been discussed between himself and the federal Minister of Justice.[38] Section 98 made the Communist Party and any organizations affiliated to the party or controlled or led by party members *de facto* illegal in Ontario and any other province where the provincial authorities chose to enforce it. Frank Scott, the McGill University civil liberties expert, pointed out in 1932 that Canada was the only liberal democracy then in existence where the Communist Party was illegal.[39]

Labour historians have claimed that the main reason for the use of Section 98 against the communists was to cripple attempts by the Workers' Unity League to organize the unemployed.[40] There seems little doubt of this considering the emphasis placed on the alleged dangers of the WUL in the pamphlet published under the auspices of W.H. Price. The successful use of Section 98 was an intimidating factor in dealing with the organized unemployed. The section of the Act providing for the prosecution of persons who had attended meetings of an "unlawful" association, distributed its literature or spoke publicly in its support and could not prove that they were not members of such an association placed a vast array of activities on the verge of illegality. This uncertainty was meant to act as a deterrent to persons joining a protest organization—the organization might at any time be declared an unlawful association. The same could apply to attending meetings or demonstrations sponsored by organizations which the authorities might consider covered by Section 98.

Yet their strategy did not bring the desired results. The unemployed organizations continued to grow and their militancy increased during 1931. With the employment situation becoming steadily worse, the arrests and increased intimidation appear to have had only a marginal effect, if at all. In late 1931 the government responded by stepping up raids on the offices of unemployed associations, but this as well seems to have had little effect on the extent of unrest and the activities of the organized unemployed.

Throughout the latter half of 1931, while the Ontario government was busy arresting and prosecuting the communist leaders, the federal government occupied itself with preparing for more drastic actions should the situation call for it. In June there had been a meeting of General McNaughton, Chief of the General Staff, and several of his staff at which plans were made for calling out the Non-Permanent Active Militia (NPAM) and the Permanent Force in aid to the civil power should it be considered necessary.[41]

> The C.G.S. stated that it might be necessary in the course of the late summer to provide for the calling out and organization of some 20,000 all ranks of the Non-Permanent Active Militia, and that these troops when called out might probably be on duty for some considerable time.[42]

It was proposed that special service companies from militia regiments be used and that recruiting be stepped up. Later in the year military officials began laying plans for using the navy and air force in aid to the civil power.[43]

The federal government also adopted a more ambitious programme for deporting radical immigrants. On October 13, 1931, a meeting was held in the office of the Minister of Justice for the purpose of discussing this subject.[44] The importance of the meeting was attested to by the rank of those attending: Honourable W.A. Gordon, Acting Minister of Justice; Honourable D.M. Sutherland, Minister of National Defence; A.L. Jaliffe, Commissioner of Immigration; Major-General J.H. MacBrien, Commissioner of the RCMP; and Major-General A.G.L. McNaughton, Chief of the General Staff. It was decided at the meeting that the army would turn Melville Island Barracks at Halifax over to the RCMP to be used as a detention centre for those awaiting deportation.

Meanwhile, the RCMP began to prepare themselves for a greater role in suppressing disturbances. The General Staff issued 300 bayonets and 30,000 rounds of .303 ammunition to the RCMP at Regina.[45] A bayonet instructor was also dispatched to the RCMP in Regina and bayonet instructors were placed at the disposal of the force in Winnipeg and Vancouver. There were also arrangements to make the Minto Armoury in Winnipeg available for the accommodation of fifty to one hundred RCMP members. It appears that the RCMP and military officials feared major outbreaks in various parts of the country but particularly in the West.

The year 1931 had been a year of worsening economic conditions, more militant protests by the organized unemployed and bitter and violent trade union struggles such as the Estevan-Bienfait coal miners' strike. It also saw the greatest use of political repression since the Winnipeg General Strike of 1919. The authorities were obviously fearful of even more unrest and were preparing more political repression to deal with it.

Footnotes

1. Public Archives of Canada (PAC), *Bennett Papers*, M-1453, Vol. 798, 394, p. 493597.
2. *Bennett Papers*, File No. U-125, January-April, 1935, p. 4905791. Statement by Perley on April 26, 1935.
3. *Bennett Papers*, M-1086, pp. 262360-63. Bennett to W.R. Givens of Kingston, September 30, 1933.
4. Montreal *Gazette*, August 13, 1913.
5. Toronto *Mail and Empire*, February 5, 1931.
6. *Ibid.* An excellent discussion of civil liberties controversies raging in Toronto at the time of Mulock's speech is contained in "Liberty and Authority: Civil Liberties in Toronto, 1929-1935" by S.M. Skebo, an unpublished M.A. thesis completed at the University of British Columbia in 1968.
7. Toronto *Mail and Empire*, February 5, 1931.
8. H.M. Cassidy, *Unemployment and Relief in Ontario, 1929-1932.* (Toronto and Vancouver: J. M. Dent and Sons, Ltd., 1932), p. 253.
9. *Canadian Annual Review (CAR)*, 1932, p. 419.
10. *CAR*, 1933, p. 109.
11. *Statistics of Canada*, 1919, Vols. I and II, p. 107.
12. House of Commons *Debates*, 1932, Vol. III, pp. 2658-59, 2638-88, 2716.
13. There are several accounts of politically motivated deportations during these years in the Toronto *Star, Canadian Forum* and *Canadian Labour Defender*, which was the official organ of the Canadian Labour Defense League, an organization specializing in defending political prisoners.
14. *Canadian Forum*, February 1934.
15. The figures from 1931 to 1933 are taken from the *Canadian Annual Review* for these years. The figure of 25,000 for the previous thirty years is from a statement by the Minister of Immigration, quoted in *Canadian Annual Review*, 1930-31, p. 575 as follows: "An examination of the published reports shows that in the past 30 years deportations have totalled upwards of 25,000 to all countries."

16. Toronto *Mail and Empire,* April 11, 1932.
17. *Canadian Annual Review,* 1930-31, pp. 453-54.
18. *Ibid.*
19. *Ibid.*
20. Toronto *Telegram* quoted in S.M. Skebo, "Liberty and Authority: Civil Liberties in Toronto, 1929-1935" (unpublished M.A. thesis, University of British Columbia, 1968).
21. Stuart Jamieson, *Times of Trouble: Labour Unrest and Industrial Conflict in Canada, 1900-1966,* Study No. 22, Task Force on Labour Relations, 1966-68, Information Canada, 1971.
22. PAC, *Bennett Papers,* Film No. 395, Vol. 1454, MacBrien's statement is referred to in a letter from Norman F. Priestley, Vice-President of the United Farmers of Alberta, to Prime Minister Bennett, July 25, 1935.
23. PAC, *Bennett Papers.*
24. PAC, *Department of Defence Papers,* Confidential Memorandum signed by General McNaughton and distributed to the Adjutant-General; Quarter-Master General; D.O.C., M.D. No. 71; Deputy Minister of Labour; Prime Minister's Secretary; and Commissioner of the RCMP, May 29, 1935.
25. *Ibid.*
26. *Ibid.*
27. PAC, *Bennett Papers,* M-989, Film No. 83, Lockwood to Bennett, June 26, 1935.
28. *Ibid.*
29. *Bennett Papers,* Bennett to Lockwood, July 8, 1935.
30. *Ibid.*
31. *Bennett Papers,* Vol. 484, Arcand to Bennett, May 22, 1930, quoted in *The Swastika and the Maple Leaf* by Lita-Rose Betcherman, Fitzhenry and Whiteside, 1975, p. 10.
32. Betcherman, *op. cit.,* p. 10.
33. *Ibid.,* p. 38.
34. *Ibid.,* p. 42.
35. *Statistics of Canada,* 1919, Vols. I and II, p. 308.
36. Frank R. Scott, "The Trial of the Toronto Communists," *Queen's Quarterly,* 1932.
37. *Ibid.*
38. Copies of the booklets are contained in the *Bennett Papers,* PAC, M-1314; Film No. 310, pp. 388406-24.
39. *Canadian Annual Review,* 1932, p. 425.
40. Scott, *op. cit.*
41. Jamieson, *op. cit.,* pp. 235-36.
42. PAC, *McNaughton Papers,* Vol. 10, File 46, CGS Memorandum (Secret), June 13, 1931.
43. *Ibid.*
44. *McNaughton Papers,* Memorandum of CGS to CRTC, October 27, 1931.
45. *McNaughton Papers,* Vol. 10, File No. 46, Secret Memorandum of CGS to Adjutant-General, October 14, 1931.

CHAPTER III

The Establishment of
Relief Camps

Despite all the effort put into cracking down on agitators and the disaffected, the unrest did not subside during 1931 and 1932. And the large numbers of single, transient unemployed were the people feared most of all by the authorities. The possibility of being cut off relief, imprisoned or deported was of much more concern to the married unemployed, who had the fate of their immediate families to consider. The single, homeless unemployed were not so easily intimidated, and they received minimal relief assistance in any case. Even the threat of imprisonment began to lose its deterrent effect to hungry men in a cold Canadian winter. The prison system could not possibly have accommodated the numbers involved in any event.

The problem of what to do about the single unemployed was further complicated because neither the municipalities nor the provinces nor the federal government wanted to assume responsibility for them. Public opinion and the threat of disorder compelled some provinces in 1931 and 1932 to take measures beyond the mere provision of soup kitchens and hostels.

Saskatchewan, where many of the municipalities were financially insolvent, was the first province to establish work camps where the single unemployed could get room and board and a nominal wage in the neighbourhood of $5.00 per month.[1] The camps were virtually compulsory for many unattached men. They were denied relief in the cities and towns and forced to keep moving, face arrest for vagrancy, or go to the camps.

Alberta established a similar system of work camps. British Columbia, where the numbers of transient unemployed relative to the population was greatest, established both work camps and "holding camps" where the single unemployed could be housed and fed and paid a small allowance while they waited for the chance of a job.[2] The Ontario government employed a few single unemployed on northern road construction relief projects.

None of the provinces built facilities anywhere near adequate to handle the situation. Unrest continued to build in the cities. The camps which did exist, with their nominal "wages" and, in the case of the holding camps, sheer boredom, were intensely unpopular with the unemployed and quickly became centres of protest. The provinces, and particularly British Columbia with its influx of unemployed from the Prairies, were pressing the Bennett government to do something about the "single homeless unemployed male" population.

General McNaughton toured the country during the summer and fall of 1932 and was appalled. McNaughton observed the deteriorating health of the transient unemployed and concluded that much of the productive labour force of the country was being destroyed. "We were destroying, physically and mentally, the very best of our people, the people that we would need the moment we got over this temporary depression—and to get the economy on the rails again."[3] By the fall of 1932 this was a concern being expressed by an increasing number of editorialists, politicians and officials of social agencies.

McNaughton had other reasons for concern. As Chief of the General Staff, he would be the one person in the country most directly responsible for restoring order should unrest in the large urban centres lead to insurrection, general strikes or other forms of upheaval. The prospect of using the army to aid the civil power was not looked upon with favour by McNaughton. He may have been an authoritarian but he was a professional soldier who took no pleasure in making war on civilian populations.

It was McNaughton who devised the scheme of establishing relief camps for the single unemployed under the auspices of the Department of Defence. These would help preserve the labour force and maintain order, but he had an additional motive. A relief camp system operated by the Department of Defence could provide administrative experience for armed forces personnel and it would enable the Department to construct military installations at a minimal cost which would otherwise probably not be built at all.[4] This was particularly important when the state of the economy and public anti-military sentiment made it difficult for governments to justify increased military expenditures.

McNaughton sold the idea of military operated relief camps to the federal Commissioner of Unemployment Relief and the Minister of Labour, who together won the support of the Bennett Cabinet. The result was an Order-in-Council of October 8, 1932, authorizing the Department of Defence to establish a system of work camps for the accommodation of physically fit, single, homeless males. The scheme would be carried on under the authority of successive Orders-in-Council until the federal relief camp system was abolished in 1936. The relief camp system was to be nominally responsible to the Department of Labour but was administered by the Department of Defence and more specifically by General McNaughton and his General Staff.

It is clear from government memoranda and correspondence that the purpose of the camps was to remove the single unemployed from the cities to prevent them from becoming politically organized. This is perhaps best summed up by R.K. Finlayson, Assistant to the Prime Minister.

> It would be a great mistake to lose sight of the main objective that the government has in this work, namely to keep urban centres clear from such single men as more readily become amenable to the designs of agitators.[5]

The military officials kept their purpose constantly in mind. McNaughton explains why the Department should not meet a request from Golden, British Columbia, for an additional relief camp in the vicinity.

> As far as my information goes I think we have quite enough camps now in the Kootenays to handle the situation as it develops. Our purpose is not to attempt to care for 100 per cent of the single homeless men but to reduce the numbers in the larger centres of population to the point that they do not constitute a menace to the civil authorities.[6]

The large camps were therefore located in relation to specific metropolitan centres or areas of unrest. Thus Petawawa military camp with accommodation for 1,081 men was used mainly for the single unemployed from Montreal.[7] Lac Seul camp near the northwest shore of Lake Superior could accommodate 1,956 men and was designed to relieve the situation in Winnipeg.[8] Other large camps included Dundurn and Val Cartier to service Saskatchewan and

Quebec City, respectively. In British Columbia, with its large concentration of single unemployed and history of working-class radicalism, there were forty-seven active projects which could accommodate 10,617 men by June 30, 1934. Most were engaged in highway construction and forestry in the B.C. interior. It was also general policy to locate camps in wilderness areas where the inmates could not easily keep in contact with the cities.

The relief camps were intended to be *de facto* compulsory for large numbers of single unemployed. Legally the camps were voluntary and the federal government continued to insist publicly that this was official policy for the duration of the relief camp scheme. People would, according to publicly announced official policy, be admitted to the camps if they personally requested the permission of the camp officials or the Employment Service of Canada or were referred by provincial or municipal authorities. It was not true that the camps were strictly voluntary—and most of the unemployed and much of the public knew it. It was this discrepancy between professed government policy and government action which helped undermine confidence in the Bennett government, defeat most of the provincial governments in the country, and undermine confidence in governmental initiative generally.

The actual manner in which the system operated was that provincial and municipal authorities refused relief to able-bodied single unemployed males and insisted they go to the camps or be arrested for vagrancy. The RCMP and other police forces, meanwhile, reversed their previous policy of virtually ignoring the illegal practice of "riding the rods."[9] It was therefore extremely difficult, if not impossible, for thousands of the single unemployed to avoid going to relief camps.

The camps were extremely unpopular with the unemployed and federal authorities often had to exert pressure on provincial and municipal officials to compel them to take a hard line in cutting off relief. Brigadier J. Sutherland Brown, District Officer Commanding of Military District 11 in B.C., warned in early 1933 that "It will be a tremendous and possibly impossible job to get the unemployed out of the cities without very powerful legal authority."[10] There were frequent consultations between provincial authorities and military officials in which the latter exerted pressure to get the unemployed out of particular towns and cities. One such was a meeting between H.H. Mathews, DOC of Military District 13, Lt. Col. E.W. Pope, and R.H. Poxley, Attorney General of B.C.[11] The military officials secured agreement from Poxley that single unemployed still on relief in Nelson would be cut off and

50

the local soup kitchen closed in an effort to force the men into the camps. More police would be sent into the area to maintain order when the relief was cut off. Mathews noted that he and his officials had succeeded in hardening the attitude of the provincial government and predicted that it would bring the desired results. "Once it is made plain the Government means business, I fancy there will be very little real trouble." [12]

Mathews was also to complain that Vancouver city officials were not sufficiently enthusiastic about arresting alleged troublemakers among the unemployed and secured assurances from Attorney-General Poxley that British Columbia would act with more vigour in the future. [13] General McNaughton would later complain about what he alleged to be the undue leniency of the courts towards vagrancy and suggest that they impose the maximum penalty of six months imprisonment on convicted vagrants. [14]

THE NATURE OF THE CAMPS

One must examine the nature of the relief camp system to understand why the camps were so intensely unpopular with the single unemployed. The fact that they were operated by the military aroused suspicion from the beginning. The camp administrators did not wear army uniforms and the strict army code of discipline was not in force, but the rules were to a considerable extent based on the code and denied the camp inmates many of the civil rights to which they were accustomed in civilian life. Section 353 of the Policy and Instructions for the Administration of Unemployment Relief Camps for Single Homeless and Unemployed Men reads as follows:

> The following rules regarding complaints will be observed:
> (a) One of the fundamental and most necessary rules for the administration of Unemployment Relief Camps is to forbid anything bearing the appearance of combination to obtain redress of alleged grievances. Appeals for redress by means of any document bearing the signature of more than one complainant, or by organized committees combining to make a complaint, are strictly forbidden.
> (b) If any man has a complaint or accusation to bring against a member of the supervisory or Administrative Staff, such complaint should be laid before the Camp Foreman, who, if necessary, will transmit it to District Headquarters or Camp Superintendent.

(c) If the Camp Foreman neglects or refuses to attend to a complaint, the complainant may bring the matter to the notice of the District Headquarters or Camp Superintendent.

(d) The Department will not countenance any steps to bring accusations before the tribunal of public opinion, either by speeches, or letters inserted in the newspapers, by men actively employed on Relief Work. Such a proceeding is a glaring violation of the rules and shows a contempt for properly constituted authority.

(e) It is the duty of the Camp Foreman to investigate all complaints, and, when receiving complains for transmission to superior authority, to point out to the parties concerned any irregularity in the means they employ in seeking redress. In hearing complaints or statements, etc., Camp Foremen are advised to invariably have another member of the Supervisory Staff present as a witness to all proceedings. The complaint, when forwarded to District Headquarters or Camp Superintendent, is to be accompanied by a statement and recommendations, if any, of the Camp Foreman.

(f) No application or complaint should ever be made to the Civil Power, except through the Camp Foreman or with his sanction. [15]

The above rules were strictly enforced and supervisory personnel who disregarded them were disciplined and sometimes dismissed. A case in point is that of D.S.B. McAllister-Thompson, a sub-foreman on Project 52 at Winterburn, Alberta. McAllister-Thompson was appointed through the intercession of General McNaughton but was later fired on suspicion of being disloyal and taking up the complaints of the men. Lieutenant-Colonel B.J. MacDonald reported to McNaughton that the foreman, Lieutenant-Colonel P. Anderson, suspected McAllister-Thompson of being an undesirable influence in the camp. "He [Anderson] stated that McAllister-Thompson although a former officer was a Union man of Socialistic tendencies probably not in sympathy with the established order." [16]

McNaughton and his officers were especially averse to dealing in any way with representatives or committees chosen by the men. Such committees were invariably regarded as subversive of constituted authority and any officers who thought otherwise were brought back into line. In a memorandum to the Minister of National Defence concerning major disturbances at Long Branch Camp in Ontario, Mcnaughton blamed the trouble partially on the leniency of the District Officer Commanding (DOC)

because his reports show that for some time before the Staff at M.D. 2 were aware of this organization of Camp Committees and that on occasions they had dealings with the men through them in absolute disregard of the specific instructions which had been given. This has been brought to the attention of all concerned, both in M.D. 2 and elsewhere, so that the error may not be repeated. [17]

There were things other than the authoritarian regulations which almost guaranteed that the camps would become unpopular. The inmates were expected to work eight hours a day for their food, lodging, work clothing where necessary, and an "allowance" of twenty cents a day. Later, a tobacco ration was also allowed after protests from inmates. The twenty cents a day was the insult which occasioned the most protest and became to the unemployed a symbol of the meanness of the Bennett government.

The physical conditions of the camps were the subject of considerable complaint. These varied a great deal but apparently were no worse than most privately operated work camps of the time, as government spokesmen never tired of reminding their critics. But privately operated work camps of the day were extremely primitive relative to urban living conditions and many men in relief camps had been accustomed to an urban environment. Even those accustomed to camp life would, if employed in the private sector, at least be working for the "going wage" and could look forward to accumulating a "stake" which could be spent in the city at a later time. In the relief camps the "allowance" of twenty cents per day was obviously instrumental in destroying morale. [18]

The provision of food in the relief camps was based on standard army rations—sufficient to maintain people in a healthy condition but usually monotonous and not enough for men who performed heavy labour. Further, even good food was liable to be ruined by poor cooks. There were frequent complaints about both quality and quantity. [19] The food costs per man day were exceptionally low, ranging from nineteen cents to twenty-two cents: for a small additional cost the Department of National Defence (DND) could have improved upon the army ration.

In addition to the DND camps there were a few camps operated by the Department of the Interior in the vicinity of national parks, where there was generally more and better food. The inmates frequently demanded that the DND camps be brought up to their standards; however, General McNaughton, obsessed with economy, responded to these demands by complaining of the "unnecessary extravagance" of the Department of the Interior camps and demanding that they reduce their rations to DND standards. [20] It was also the policy of National Defence Headquarters (NDHQ) that extras for special occasions such as Christmas come either from public donations or by cutting regular rations so as to accumulate some surplus. It was petty stinginess of this nature which further alienated the single unemployed.

Probably a greater contributing factor to camp discontent, however, was the fact that the work was performed by very primitive methods. This was a conscious policy designed to save money on machinery and equipment and to stretch out the work. It did nothing for the morale of the men to work for twenty cents per day on jobs which they knew could have been done more efficiently by machines. This was work for work's sake which might have been made somewhat more tolerable if the remuneration had been closer to normal rates of pay. It showed up in the mens' work efficiency.[21]

Other factors contributing to the discontent were the type and location of projects undertaken by DND camp workers. Of the 108 active DND projects on June 30, 1934, forty-one involved highway construction (mainly in the B.C. interior), thirty-four constructing landing fields, twelve constructing military bases, and the remainder were involved in constructing municipal airports, aerodromes and on forestry and other projects.[22] Most of these projects would normally involve heavy machinery and would not be done by hand labour. Many were also directly or indirectly related to the military. And most were located in wilderness areas or rural settings readily accessible to cities only by automobile, if at all. Some work camps were virtually snow-bound for months at a time.

Large numbers of the relief camp residents were men in their early twenties who, under normal circumstances, could have looked forward to getting jobs, marrying and raising families. Now, at a time when they were just starting adult life, there were no jobs available and the future looked bleak indeed. Many had been in and out of soup kitchens, hostels and provincial camps since 1930. Now they were being shoved aside in relief camps which the authorities claimed were "temporary" pending the opening of jobs in the private sector. Existing in what appeared to be a hopeless situation in remote camps led to boredom and frustration—and this could quickly turn to anger and outrage if conditions did not improve. When conditions indeed did not improve, the relief camps—far from promoting political stability—became training schools for radicals.

Footnotes

1. Alma Lawton, "Relief Administration in Saskatoon During the Depression," *Saskatchewan History,* Vol. XXII.
2. The horrors of the twentieth century have changed the meaning of many words in our language. In the early 1930s the "holding" camps were referred to by both the government and the public as "concentration"

camps, meaning camps where men were concentrated until they either got jobs or were moved to work camps. The term "concentration camp" did not have the negative connotation which it acquired later because of the horrors of Nazi slave camps and death camps.

3. General McNaughton, interview for CBC Archives, December 8, 1965. Quoted in John Swettenhan, *McNaughton,* Vol. I (Toronto: Ryerson Press, 1968), p. 270.

4. Swettenham, *op. cit.,* pp. 272, 274.

5. Public Archives of Canada (PAC), *Bennett Papers,* micro. p. 494237, R.K. Finlayson to A.E. Millar, October 6, 1933. The *Bennett Papers* contain many memos and letters emphasizing the same point. They include Hugh G. Farthing to A.E. Millar (P.M.'s Secretary) on September 7 and 8, 1933; Mayor Andrew Davison of Calgary to A.E. Millar, October 6, 1933. Also see Regina *Leader-Post* for May 11, 1933, for statement by Premier Anderson about Saskatoon unemployed being forced to go to Dundurn relief camp.

6. PAC, *McNaughton Papers,* Vol. 58, File 361, Vol. 2, CGS to DOC 13, December 14, 1934.

7. PAC, *Department of National Defence Papers,* General Review of the Department of National Defence Unemployment Relief Scheme, DND confidential memorandum for information of Government of Canada, August 1934.

8. *Ibid.*

9. This became general policy throughout the country except in the West during spring and fall. Certain numbers of unemployed who had spent the winter in B.C. camps would be allowed to ride the rods back to the Prairies in the spring in the hope of obtaining farm work. The policy would be relaxed again in the fall to get people into the Prairies for harvest and back to B.C. so as to clear out the Prairie cities for the winter.

10. *McNaughton Papers,* Vol. I, File 361, J.S. Brown to Secretary, DND, May 24, 1933. Brown tried without success to persuade the DND to pay wages in the camps and be less authoritarian in administration. He later left the military in protest against their relief camp policy.

11. *McNaughton Papers,* Vol. 41, 314, Vol. I, H.H. Mathews, DOC, M.D. 13 to McNaughton, July 18, 1933.

12. *Ibid.*

13. *Ibid.*

14. *McNaughton Papers,* Series II, Vol. 57, McNaughton to A.E. Millar, March 2, 1934.

15. *Department of National Defence Papers,* Unemployment Relief, Policy and Instructions for the Administration of Unemployment Relief Camps for Single Homeless and Unemployed Men.

16. *Bennett Papers,* File No. 495149, Lieutenant Colonel D.J. MacDonald to CGS, March 31, 1934.

17. *Bennett Papers,* File No. 494777, McNaughton to Minister of National Defence, October 10, 1933.

18. The twenty cents per day issue was emphasized repeatedly in *The Unemployed Worker* and other organs of the Relief Camp Workers' Union and the Workers' Unity League. It was also mentioned frequently in McNaughton's files as a cause of disturbances in the camps.

19. *McNaughton Papers,* File 359, Vol. I, Chart compiled by McNaughton on relief camp disturbances and their cause.

20. *McNaughton Papers,* File 377.

21. The work efficiency of relief camp workers across the country was found to be only 48.7% that of ordinary labour employed at prevailing rates and it was found that overall efficiency dropped as time passed. See G.M. Lefresne, *The Royal Twenty Centers: The Department of National Defence and Federal Unemployment Relief 1932-1936,* unpublished B.A. thesis, Royal Military College, Kingston, 1962, p. 179, cited in Lorne Brown, "Unemployment Relief Camps in Saskatchewan, 1933-1936," *Saskatchewan History,* Vol. XXIII, Autumn, 1970, p. 91. For a discussion of the question of whether to pay wages in the camps, see Lorne Brown, *The Bennett Government, Political Stability and the Politics of the Unemployment Relief Camps, 1930-1935,* unpublished Ph.D. thesis, Queen's University, 1979, pp. 527-29.

22. *DND Papers,* General Review of Department of National Defence Unemployment Relief Scheme, DND confidential memorandum for information of Government of Canada, August 1934.

CHAPTER IV

Conflict in the Camps

Considering the context within which they were begun, and the nature of their administration, it should have been obvious from the beginning that the relief camps would be troublesome institutions. A perceptive and sensitive government would have recognized this, but the Bennett government was not known for these qualities. They neither looked seriously at alternatives to the relief camps nor moved to make any significant administrative changes from the time the camp system was established in late 1932 until the Bennett government was defeated in 1935.

The DND relief camps were centres of controversy and conflict from the day they were established. This was especially the case in British Columbia where the unemployed were the best organized and by 1932 had already forced some minor concessions from the provincial and municipal authorities. The single unemployed in B.C. therefore probably received better treatment than elsewhere in Canada.

Before the establishment of federal camps destitute single men in B.C. had been looked after by the Special Relief Commission, a provincial agency headed by Mr. R.G. Fordham and generally referred to as the Fordham Commission. This Commission had, since 1930, operated both work camps and holding camps throughout the province. In the holding camps the men received board and lodging, medical care, clothing where necessary and a tobacco allowance. In the work camps they received an additional $7.50 per month. [1]

The unemployed in British Columbia were organized in both the cities and the provincial relief camps. From 1931 they put out a regular newsletter, *The Unemployed Worker,* which was distributed throughout the province. Demonstrations and strikes on relief projects were fairly common and were often well coordinated and provided with moral and financial support from trade unions. Many relief camps had "camp committees" which were granted what could be termed *de facto* recognition in negotiations with the project supervisors. In a few instances these committees seem to have virtually run the camps and the administrators had little choice but to accept the situation.[2] Many of these concessions had been won after militant struggles and would not be given up without a sustained fight in any new scheme inaugurated by the federal government.

The governments of Canada and British Columbia concluded an agreement on November 1, 1932, updated on May 1, 1933, under which the federal government would assume most of the financial responsibility for those physically fit, single, homeless, unemployed men who could be housed in work camps. While the agreement made this class of individuals a federal responsibility, the understanding was that the camps run by the Fordham Commission would continue to operate, with federal financial assistance, and would be supplemented by camps operated directly under the Department of National Defence.

The problem with this dual system from the point of view of DND officials was that the rations allowances and disciplining regulations were more generous and liberal in the camps operated by the Fordham Commission than in the Department of National Defence camps. The single unemployed, who were demanding work and wages rather than relief camps to begin with, would in no way accept DND camps with less food, smaller allowances and stricter regulations. Provincial officials understood this and so did some of the more perceptive military officers on the scene in British Columbia. Thus Brigadier J. Sutherland Brown, the local District Officer Commanding (DOC), pleaded with his superiors at National Defence Headquarters (NDHG) to increase cash allowances and food rations in order to avoid serious trouble.

> I am of the opinion, and the Provincial authorities agree, that any reduction of the present provincial scale would cause disappointment, probably resulting in a refusal to work—The proposed allowance of 20 cents per day for six days a week is appreciably less than the $7.50 per month at present paid by Provincial authorities to men working. The recent announcement in the daily press that the President of the U.S.A. suggested an allowance of $1.00 per day to unemployed working on government projects is a factor which may tend to cause discontent. In view of these

considerations I would stress again the undesirability of lowering in any way the present standard of feeding in camps. A reduced allowance, increased work and a reduced ration would give the malcontents and agitators with communistic leanings an excellent opportunity to cause trouble.[3]

The DND authorities not only paid no heed to J. Sutherland Brown's advice but they insisted that the Fordham Commission adhere to DND standards instead. The federal government requested, through R.W. Bruhn, Minister of Public Works for British Columbia, that the Fordham Commission continue to operate relief camps on an identical basis to the DND. They refused to change their own methods of operation but apparently wanted to share the political fallout. The B.C. government, though also Conservative at the time, was more attuned to public opinion. They would soon have an election to fight and they had learned from experience that the organized unemployed were not without support from the public. The Fordham Commission agreed to continue operating relief camps but only under their own conditions and Bruhn so informed the federal government.

> We are prepared to function only on the same lines as we have done in the past and we are not prepared to alter the rations of the camps which are to be under our control in any way shape or form.[4]

Bennett's ministers refused to listen to their fellow Conservatives and insisted that the provincial camps be operated their way or not at all.

> If Commission unwilling to continue their public service on this basis we are prepared to recommend that you dissolve Commission at once and having regard to fact that Dominion bearing entire cost we are prepared to assume the responsibility.[5]

The result of the disagreement between the Bennett government and the Fordham Commission was that the latter discontinued the operation of relief camps and most of the camps formerly administered by them were integrated into the DND system. This occasioned much criticism from the unemployed organizations and from several other sources as well. One immediate result was a strike in a number of the camps in early July, 1933, under the auspices of the British Columbia Relief Camp Workers' Union which was just then in the process of being organized and would soon evolve into the national

Relief Camp Workers' Union (RCWU) which would be in the forefront of the struggles inside and outside the relief camps for the next two years. The RCWU was affiliated to the Workers' Unity League.

The strike was directed against what *The Unemployed Worker* described as "the militarization of the camps."[6] The strike gained moral and financial support not only from the Workers' Unity League but also from a few local trade unions of the mainstream variety, a few clergymen, including Reverend Andrew Roddan, a well known United Church minister in Vancouver, and some elements of the Socialist Party of Canada and the CCF. These sympathizers could be described as the advanced guard of what would become within eighteen months very broad public support for the cause of the single unemployed. There was even some sympathy within the military and at least one prominent defector who could no longer abide the role he was expected to play. Brigadier J. Sutherland Brown, after failing to convince General McNaughton to adopt a more generous policy towards rations and allowances, resigned from the Army and publicly criticized the Department of National Defence and federal relief policy generally.[7]

The strike itself lasted only a few days and involved fewer than 500 workers. The relief camp workers were not yet sufficiently organized to carry on large and sustained actions. But these events were an indication of the shape of things to come. There were similar and larger strikes in the B.C. camps in August and September, 1933, and nearly every month thereafter for the next two years.

The DND relief camps got off to an equally rocky start in several other provinces. In Alberta, where there was a United Farmers of Alberta government, there were federal-provincial tensions over federal policy towards the unemployed and much criticism of the federal government in the press.[8] There was also considerable trouble forcing the single unemployed from Edmonton to enter the camps.

In Saskatchewan the DND erected a large camp at Dundurn, near Saskatoon, where single men would be employed erecting a large militia camp. This was begun at the urgent request of the provincial Conservative government after overcrowding and unrest at a provincial relief camp on the outskirts of Saskatoon led to a major confrontation with police on May 8, 1933, which resulted in the death of one RCMP officer and injuries to several other policemen and unemployed civilians.[9] Premier Anderson made it clear from the beginning that the single unemployed from the Saskatoon camp would be compelled to go to the DND project at Dundurn or face dire consequences.

60

> If the men from this camp refused to go (and they thought the
> majority would go) the city would be advised to furnish no relief
> and the police would be ordered to deal severely with begging
> and vagrancy. [10]

Twenty-six people were brought to trial on charges emanating from
the May 8 disturbances and the trials became a *cause célèbre* among
left-wing circles in the province.

A similar pattern emerged in Ontario. The relief camp scheme
was inaugurated amidst much public criticism and resistance from
the single unemployed. As early as September 15, 1933, a well
organized and determined strike broke out at Long Branch, a large
relief camp of 700 people engaged in forest conservation work. [11]
As was always the case, the camp officials responded by ordering
the men to return to work or be expelled. The men refused to return
without concessions and consequently the entire contingent of 700
was expelled and the camp closed. Most of the men went to Toronto
from whence they had come.

The distrust of the relief camp system increased as time passed,
and this distrust, combined with the frustration of the camp inmates,
meant that strikes and disturbances became almost a constant feature
of camp life. General McNaughton kept charts of the disturbances
in relief camps considered significant enough to be reported to
NDHQ. One chart indicated that there were fifty-seven such disturbances between June 27, 1933, and March 31, 1934. [12] In the
same period at least twenty-one camp inmates received prison sentences
for their involvement in the disturbances. Another of McNaughton's
charts reveals that a total of 3,379 men had either been expelled
for disciplinary reasons or left the camps in protest up to December
31, 1933, and most of the camps had just been opened in the spring
and summer of that year. [13] Prime Minister Bennett would later
quote figures from the Department of National Defence to the effect
that 12,601 men had been expelled from the camps for disciplinary
reasons up to late June, 1935. [14] Not a single month passed from
the time the camps were established when there were not disruptions
serious enough to be reported to NDHQ.

The reports received by McNaughton also stipulated what local
officials considered to be the reasons for disturbances and described
the nature of the disruptions and the action taken by camp officials.

The reasons cited for the disturbances were innumerable but a
few were mentioned more frequently than others. Complaints about
the quality and quantity of food were mentioned nineteen times as

being the factor or one of the factors leading to a disruption. Complaints concerning the allowance of twenty cents per day or the working hours were listed as the main factor in ten disturbances. Eleven disruptions were blamed on "agitators" or "malcontents" with no other reasons being cited. On twelve occasions men were alleged to have embarked upon a "disturbance" out of sympathy with men who had been "discharged for cause" from a particular camp. Four disruptions resulted from complaints directed against specific administrators. Complaints about unsanitary practices such as using cracked enamelware were cited as reasons for four work stoppages. [15]

In addition to the major grievances there were a host of complaints of a minor nature which cropped up from time to time as reasons for disruptions in camp routine. These included complaints about clothing, tobacco, boots, cutlery, soap, and cigarette papers. On at least six occasions the camp officials claimed that they could ascertain no reason at all for the work disruptions. They did not even point the finger at "agitators" or "malcontents." It is probable that the level of frustration was so high a specific "reason" was not really necessary.

Most of the disturbances were described as strikes or "refusal to work" on the part of either some or all of the workers in particular camps. [16] There were very few instances of actual violence or rioting. On one occasion the men were reported as having raided the cookhouse. There were a few outbreaks of minor and very brief riots during mealtime in the dining halls. The men in one camp broke all of the enamelware. In another camp they attempted to sabotage some machinery. There were very few instances of assaults on foremen and other camp officials.

The frequent strikes were obviously an indication of widespread discontent. And that there were so many work stoppages and yet so few acts of vandalism and violence is an indication of a process among the men in the camps and of the influence of the Relief Camp Workers' Union. The orderly fashion in which the strikes were carried out indicates a considerable organization and discipline among the camp workers. Although many of the strikes appear to have been spontaneous in the sense that they were "sparked" by a specific incident, often trivial in itself, the strikers generally organized themselves well and insisted that they would go back to work only if a specific demand or several demands were met.

Many of the strikes were not, of course, spontaneous in that it was agreed in advance by an "underground" leadership network that a certain camp or several camps would walk out on a particular day to press grievances which were bothering the men most at the time. The leaders of most "disturbances" obviously possessed a high degree of political maturity and sense of purpose which explains the orderliness of the majority of protests. The newsletters and leaflets distributed periodically by the Relief Camp Workers' Union repeatedly denounced individual acts of violence and discouraged adventurist tactics. They also warned again provocateurs who might wish to foment violence for their own reasons.

The Workers' Unity League, which had played such a key role in organizing urban unemployed and several provincial camps, sent organizers into the DND camps where they met with considerable success. As early as the end of 1933 military officers in British Columbia were reporting that the RCWU appeared to have an organization in almost every camp in the province.

> There is a very active organization known as the British Columbia Relief Camp Workers' Union which publishes a bulletin monthly and which in spite of all our efforts appears to reach most of our camps. I obtain copies from time to time and they indicate a pretty complete organization which has a foot-hold in practically every camp. [17]

By the end of 1934 the RCWU had managed to build some semblance of organization throughout Canada. This took tremendous dedication and skill considering that any form of organization in the camps was against DND regulations. Anyone caught attempting to organize or distributing RCWU leaflets would be expelled from camp immediately and blacklisted throughout the DND camp system. Such people would also be on blacklists in the cities which meant they would be unable to obtain relief. Many were imprisoned, usually for vagrancy. Nonetheless, the organizing continued and took the form of secret "bush committees" in the camps, which would distribute leaflets, coordinate and generalize individual grievances, and provide leadership in strikes and other actions of this nature. When they were discovered and blacklisted they would try to enter other camps under assumed names. A skillful organizer might last some months before the authorities finally caught up with him. [18]

Before long the majority of protest actions and the most effective strikes were led by supporters of the RCWU. This added to the illegitimacy of such protests in the eyes of DND officials, most of whom were obsessed with a fear of "communist agitators" and tended to blame most unrest on "subversives" exploiting minor grievances. They did not attempt to examine underlying causes. That relief camp inmates would be perfectly content but for the work of a few communists remained the official public stance of the Bennett government until its defeat in 1935. While to a large extent this argument may have been used as a mere propaganda device by politicians to discredit organized protests, it appears likely that General McNaughton and the majority of army officers genuinely believed it. It was an easy explanation to career army officers who could not understand why civilians so disliked the spartan, tightly disciplined kind of environment which they attempted to enforce in relief camps.

The fact that almost anyone who complained of conditions was likely to be labelled a communist agitator seems to have had the effect of playing into the hands of RCWU organizers. While such organizers might be regarded with hatred and contempt by the authorities, they were more likely to be looked upon with admiration by the single unemployed, and the more they were hounded by the authorities the more popular they became. James Gray, then a reporter for the Winnipeg *Free Press* who covered part of the On-to-Ottawa Trek, showed considerable insight into the psychology of the relief camps when he wrote about them years later.

> The inevitable collisions of the Communist organizers with the authorities were always a tonic for inmate morale. That one man was willing to stick his neck out on their behalf was at least passing proof that they were worth fighting for. To many of them, the Communists were the sort of men they wished they could be. [19]

The truly amazing thing about the DND administration of the relief camps was that, during two years of turmoil and struggle, very few of the top administrators appear to have learned anything about the aspirations and psychology of the men they were attempting to control. Not only did they refuse to increase allowances or food rations, they also consistently refused to consider any form of negotiations or recognition of camp committees. It does not seem to have occurred to NDHQ that there might have been more tranquility in the camps if they had made a few significant concessions or that they might be able to institutionalize and "cool out" the struggle by recognizing and negotiating with elected camp committees.

Between June 27, 1933, and March 31, 1934, there were thirty-six actions reported to NDHQ which were defined as strikes or work stoppages. On only six occasions did they make any concessions to get the men back to work. One was a simultaneous strike in five B.C. camps on September 9, 1933, in which the men demanded a free ration of tobacco. They returned to work when it was explained that tobacco would be issued when the cost of other rations permitted. Later it became DND policy to supply a free tobacco ration in all relief camps.

On two occasions drunken and incompetent supervisory personnel were fired after their behaviour sparked work stoppages. On three occasions the men returned to work after an investigation was promised into their complaints. In one of these cases "adjustments" were later made in the food ration.

The much more common means of handling work stoppages was to threaten anyone who refused to work with expulsion from the camps. This was a considerable threat, especially during the winter months, considering that those expelled from the camps had to make their way back to the cities on their own, and, further, relief would be virtually impossible to obtain in the cities. Ringleaders were often arrested on various charges and sentenced to short terms in prison as well.

Most strikes lasted a few days. They ended after several men were expelled from camp, others left in sympathy, and some of the ringleaders were arrested. A few examples will serve to illustrate the general situation. [20] On March 21, 1933, thirty men doing relief work at Royal Military College, Kingston, Ontario, refused to work on the grounds that there was too much rain. Twenty-one of the men were discharged and the remainder returned to work. An entire camp went on strike at Salmon Arm, B.C., on November 10, 1933, "in sympathy with men discharged for violence." The strike ended with twenty-three men leaving camp and the remainder returning to work. A camp on the Hope-Princeton Highway in British Columbia was struck on November 24, 1933, in sympathy with three men who had been discharged. This strike ended with forty-eight men leaving the camp. On December 1, 1933, eight men refused to work in a camp at White Rock, B.C. The eight were discharged and then twenty-three more struck in sympathy. The twenty-three were removed from the camp by the British Columbia police. On December 14, 1933, fifty men struck for more and better food and shorter working hours at a camp known as The Gap in the mountains west of Calgary. Two men were arrested, eleven were discharged, and the remainder returned to work. A strike erupted at Evansburg Camp, B.C., on February 9, 1934, over complaints about food. Thirty-seven men were discharged and one of the strike leaders, a man named Van Leary, was arrested and sentenced to three months imprisonment.

By the late winter of 1934 the men in the relief camps were becoming sufficiently well organized by the RCWU that as many as a dozen camps were going on strike simultaneously.[21] Four camps in the Nelson area and an unspecified number in the West Kootenay area of British Columbia were struck simultaneously on February 22, 1934. The trouble was blamed by military officials on "agitation by well known troublemakers" and the situation did not return to normal until nearly 100 men had been discharged or left the camps in protest.[22] On March 6, 1934, at least twelve B.C. camps were struck simultaneously in what military personnel described as agitation against "slave" camps and "militarizing" and part of a province-wide "demonstration against varied fancied grievances."[23] On this occasion at least sixty-five and possibly more than 100 men were discharged or left the camps in protest.

As the federal government refused to change their general relief strategy and as DND officials refused to alter the nature of the camps the struggle escalated and presented new problems. By 1934 the many "agitators" who had been expelled from the camps and effectively blacklisted, along with many more who had left the camps in sympathy with them, were gathering in the cities, demanding relief and continuing their agitation among the urban unemployed.

In cities like Vancouver, where the unemployed were well organized, scores of agitators and organizers, and sometimes hundreds of their sympathizers, could not obtain government relief. They were looked after by the unemployed associations, left-wing labour unions and various organizations affiliated to the Workers' Unity League. Meanwhile, they organized demonstrations to keep up the political pressure and "tin canning" and other events to raise funds.[24] Conflicts arose between local and provincial officials, who wanted these people out of the cities, and DND authorities, who would not allow them back into the camps.

Out of this conflict the DND authorities were forced to soften their policy on blacklisting those expelled from the camps. As of spring 1934 they began to make exceptions so that men who had been "discharged for cause" or left camp on their own volition during strikes, but were deemed to be followers rather than ringleaders, could return to the camps if they promised to obey camp rules. This change in policy reflected the situation after the mass strikes of February and March when hundreds had left the camps.[25]

While they were softening their policy in this one respect, federal officials were urging provincial governments to adopt more repressive measures and were also preparing more repression on their own account. Premier Pattullo of British Columbia was urged to fully enforce Section 239 of the Criminal Code dealing with vagrancy and to imprison more people under other statutes as a means of enforcing order in the cities.[26] Prime Minister Bennett emphasized the federal position on these matters in a telegram to Premier Pattullo on March 2, 1934.

> Your Attorney-General in his telegram of twenty-fourth February suggests that there is difficulty in dealing with the situation due to short sentences and jail accommodation being inadequate. I am satisfied that the law officers of the Crown can rectify the first difficulty by properly presenting the situation to the Justice before whom cases are heard and the province can provide jail accommodation to meet the situation. STOP regarding re-admittance to camps of men discharged for cause. We recognize that those numbers include men who have been misled by criminal agitators and who regret their action. We have authorized our officers to re-admit men when they are reasonably sure they will give no further cause for discharge.[27]

While putting pressure on provincial authorities and making a few minor concessions themselves, Ottawa was busy preparing very drastic measures to further curtail the civil liberties of Canadians if necessary. In fact, they had been preparing such measures since the spring of 1933 when the relief camp scheme had been underway for only a few months. General McNaughton sent the following instructions to the Quartermaster-General of the Army on April 3, 1933:

> Under the arrangements presently under consideration for the handling of unemployment relief there will be need for the establishment of certain Camps of Discipline to which persons convicted of vagrancy may be committed. It is considered that one of these camps could well be located at Fort Henry, Kingston. Would you please have this project studied confidentially by the D.O.C. M.D. 3 with a view to clearing the Fort of Ordinance Stores and Ammunition and making the necessary preliminary arrangements for accommodation.
>
> Please say the numbers that can be accommodated and the work of renovation which the prisoners could be put to. It will probably be necessary to enclose the whole Fort with barbed wire entanglements.[28]

In a memorandum later in the month to W.M. Dickson, Private Secretary to the Minister of Labour, McNaughton referred to discussions with law officers and other officials of the Department of Justice and the Department of National Defence concerning "the legal questions involved in the confinement in 'Camps of Discipline' of persons convicted of vagrancy under the amendments contemplated to Section 238 (b) of the Criminal Code."[29] The contemplated amendments would have had the effect of making it an offence for an unemployed man on relief to refuse to accept employment, if offered, on a project deemed relief work. That person, if convicted, could then be imprisoned in a "Camp of Discipline."

The government did not proceed with the amendments. The reasons for declining are not totally clear but one factor appears to have been public opinion and reaction in some circles to the case of "Regina vs. Fleury" which was fought out in the Ontario courts during April and May 1933. Joseph Fleury, a man living on public relief in a hostel in Oshawa, had refused to go to the Trenton relief camp on the grounds that the pay was insufficient and going to the camp might prevent him from getting a job. Fleury was thereupon charged with vagrancy and convicted by a police magistrate in Oshawa. On appeal the conviction was quashed. The result of the appeal drew comment in legal circles and the daily press. The Ottawa Citizen based an editorial on the case and came down on the side of Joseph Fleury and Judge Garrow who had quashed the conviction.

> Details of this important appeal are given in the current Ontario Weekly Notes, issued by the law society of Upper Canada. It is important because it reminds authorities that men on relief have still some choice left as to their movements. Judge Garrow heard the appeal and in his judgment says: "It seemed to be implied in this conviction that any unfortunate receiving relief who declines to accept the first job offered thereby became liable to conviction as a vagrant. No sympathy is to be extended to idlers willing to live at public expense, but it is still necessary that in this, as in every other case of this kind, the charge laid must be made out and proved by the prosecution."
>
> It is a good thing that this conviction was quashed, and for several reasons. It saves the operations of work camps under relief schemes from being stigmatized as forced labour. It will prevent officials from prosecuting as vagrants men who, if the conviction had been upheld, become vagrants for refusing any kind of job. And this is said in full agreement with Judge Garrow's observation

that "no sympathy is to be extended to idlers willing to live at public expense."[30]

The single unemployed had finally won an important case in the courts and were receiving at least lukewarm sympathy from some important newspapers. Public opinion was beginning to change, and this, as well as the potential legal implications had DND officials worried. As it turned out, though the Fleury case was not used later as a precedent. The *Citizen* editorial as well as other newspaper clippings about the Fleury case were placed in Mc-Naughton's files along with material relating to Camps of Discipline. They seem to have got cold feet about an ordinary amendment to the Criminal Code and decided to proceed instead under the so-called "blank cheque" provided by the Relief Act of 1933.[31]

At the end of May, 1933, government officials took additional steps to prepare for Camps of Discipline which could be put into operation and administered by an Order-in-Council under the "peace, order and good government" clause of the Relief Act of 1933.[32] After a discussion it was agreed that Plaxton and Orde would refine and work out more definite proposals.

One week later, on June 7, McNaughton instructed the Quartermaster-General to prepare a layout and specifications for a Camp of Discipline to accommodate 100 prisoners. McNaughton indicated that the matter was of some urgency and several hundred men might have to be incarcerated.

> Could this be dealt with as an urgent matter, please. Draft layout to be referred to J.A.G. and D.O.P. for comment, and to be suitable for expansion by the addition of standard units designed for 100 men under detention.[33]

An Order-in-Council was drafted so that the government could move extremely quickly to imprison people in Camps of Discipline if necessary. The draft Order-in-Council would give the government sweeping power to curtail civil liberties.[34] Under the Relief Act of 1933 it could be invoked when Parliament was not sitting. The Order-in-Council provided that unemployed people who refused to go to the regular DND relief camps, or did go but disobeyed the rules and regulations, could be imprisoned in a Camp of Discipline for up to sixty days. If there was doubt about whether a person was "unemployed and homeless" the burden of proof "shall lie upon the defendant." After a person was released from a Camp of Discipline he could, of course, be re-arrested within a short time if he still refused to go to a regular camp and remained "unemployed and homeless."

To be certain that there would be no delay should the government decide to move, arrangements were made to have copies of the draft Order-in-Council in the hands of all District Officers Commanding under cover of a secret and confidential letter. [35] In the event that the Order-in-Council was passed, the DOC's in the districts concerned would be notified by a code telegram. [36] Unless and until it was passed its existence would be kept secret.

Rules and regulations governing the internal operations of Camps of Discipline were also placed in the hands of District Officers Commanding and were extremely comprehensive. The rules and regulations were a modified version of those used in the penitentiaries of the day. [37] For instance, there were two "stages" and an inmate could move from the lower to the higher stage by accumulating marks for good behaviour, productive work, etc. The second stage included such privileges as sleeping on mattresses, receiving visitors more frequently and writing letters more often. There was a list of nineteen reasons for which an inmate could be punished. These included such things as conversing with another inmate without authority, carelessness at work, absence from Divine Service, and use of obscene language. Punishments could include solitary confinement and bread-and-water diets.

The federal government later prepared a draft Bill which could be passed by Parliament should Parliament be in session at a time when the cabinet wished to establish Camps of Discipline. The draft Bill allowed the government the same authority as the draft Order-in-Council except that one section stipulated the Act would not be invoked in any province "unless a request has been made by the Lieutenant-Governor in Council of that province to the appropriate Minister." The federal authorities were leery of invading provincial jurisdiction over the administration of justice without the consent of the provinces concerned. Ottawa could pass such laws but the provinces would have to administer them. They feared taking new drastic measures without a political base to back them up. Because of this they also decided against invoking their draft Order-in-Council without a specific request from a provincial government.

That the federal government was fully prepared to use the drastic legislative and executive measures which they had prepared was quickly illustrated during June of 1933. Controversy was raging over the phasing out of the camps run by the Fordham Commission and their replacement with federal DND camps in British Columbia. Tension was extremely high in Vancouver, and Premier Tolmie's

70

Conservative government was not only pressing the Bennett government to improve rations and allowances in the DND camps but to assume additional responsibility for the single unemployed. The federal authorities refused both requests but offered the use of military force and prison camps instead. In a telegram dated June 19, 1933, federal minister of labour W.A. Gordon reminded Premier Tolmie of the provisions of the Militia Act and the Criminal Code in respect to military aid to the Civil Power and also pointed out

> that provided you deem situation is beyond your power Dominion Government at your request signified by Order-in-Council of your Government will take special powers under the Relief Act of 1933 in respect to maintenance of Peace Order and Good Government which will permit the arrest and detention by due process of law of all persons without employment or other visible means of maintaining themselves who are eligible for our camps and who refuse employment therein. [38]

B.C. Attorney-General R.H. Poxley replied that such drastic action was neither necessary nor desirable. "Think it advisable to avoid drastic measures either under code or amendments to Relief Act." [39]

What went on between British Columbia and federal authorities over the next year reveals that public opinion was beginning to shift markedly against state authoritarianism and in favour of the rights of the unemployed. It also reveals less than a forthright approach to problems on the part of both levels of government and from both the Conservative and Liberal parties. The Bennett government was encouraging British Columbia to pass the appropriate Order-in-Council requesting the establishment of federal prison camps. A provincial election campaign was underway throughout the summer and early fall of 1933 and the Tolmie administration did not wish to be associated with new repressive manoeuvres which might alienate public opinion. The situation was complicated by the fact that the newly founded Co-operative Commonwealth Federation (CCF) was stronger in B.C. than anywhere else and unemployment issues were prominent in the campaign. Some military officials seemed to be annoyed that the public had any say in the matter at all and viewed vociferous public criticism of relief camp policy as irresponsible if not actually bordering on sedition. Thus H.H. Mathews, the temporary replacement for J. Sutherland Brown after the latter resigned as DOC for Military District 11, reported to McNaughton in July 1933 that the provincial election campaign was inhibiting freedom of action by the state.

I doubt if any drastic steps will be taken by the Provincial authorities to force men who refuse to work in correction camps, or whatever such establishments might be called, while the election campaign is on. The "iron heel of military despotism" and "slave camps" are not pleasant sounding diatribes to meet on the hustings in times like these, and will be avoided as much as possible, I fancy, by local constitutional political parties.[40]

While local Conservative politicians were careful not to be publicly associated with more repressive measures during the election campaign, they were privately urging their federal colleagues to "throw the book" at alleged agitators and troublemakers, if the action in question could be done speedily and quietly. W.G. Beeman of the B.C. military district described to his superiors a conversation he had with B.C. Attorney-General R.H. Poxley, who was either unaware that Ottawa had been pursuing a policy very similar to what he recommended since at least 1932 or thought that it needed tightening up even more.[41]

The Tolmie administration was defeated in the autumn election and the federal authorities found themselves faced with an even more sensitive situation in British Columbia. Duff Pattullo, the new Liberal premier, was a maverick populist who claimed to be a fighter for the underdog and a champion of the people against the big vested interests but who possessed an authoritarian streak with an attachment to state authority and no nonsense "law and order." He represented the first of a particular type of politician produced by the turmoil of the 1930s and closely resembled his fellow Liberal, Mitch Hepburn, in Ontario; "Bible Bill" Aberhart of Alberta Social Credit; and Maurice Duplessis, Union Nationale premier of Québec.

The Pattullo forces had made much of the employment situation during the election campaign. They did not promise many specific programmes themselves but demanded that the federal government undertake massive public works projects to provide jobs. They also demanded that Ottawa bear more of the cost of unemployment relief and the entire cost of relief for the single unemployed regardless of whether they were in DND camps. They constantly pointed out that many of the British Columbia unemployed had migrated from other parts of Canada.

Once in office the Pattullo government put much more emphasis on demanding federal action than they did in implementing economic changes of their own. They argued that they could do little to influence the economy themselves anyway and unemployment should be a federal responsibility. Their incessant pressure on the Bennett government made political points with the public. They were privately urging repressive measures by the federal government, however, providing they themselves were not implicated. For its part, Ottawa maintained a consistent position of refusing additional expenditures, encouraging the provinces to fully enforce existing laws, and offering to undertake more repressive measures themselves but only if the provincial government would officially and publicly take joint responsibility for them.

The two levels of government began an extended and private exchange of views in early December, 1933, about the most appropriate means of controlling the single unemployed and particularly whether "special" camps should be established and, if so, who should take responsibility for them. G.S. Pearson, minister of labour in the Pattullo government, began the exchange by complaining about the old problem of men who were expelled from the camps congregating in the cities where they were perceived as a threat to public order. Pearson suggested what would be in effect prison camps. "We suggest for your consideration that there must be some way by which this class can be disciplined by the establishment of special camps in which the worst cases could be placed."[42]

The Bennett government, which had been urging Tolmie to take such action the previous June, was now more cautious. W.A. Gordon replied to Pearson on behalf of Ottawa and suggested stricter enforcement of the regular Criminal Code before resorting to more drastic action.

> I would suggest before setting up further disciplinary machinery as proposed by you that more effective administration of the law by the Provincial authorities would in all probability bring about the desired result. If not, it would then be soon enough to consider the steps suggested, which course should not be invoked except only as a last resort as the invocation virtually means that your Province is either unable or is failing to administer the law.[43]

As the Pattullo regime continued to insist on drastic federal action during December, 1933, and January, 1934, federal authorities took the attitude that British Columbia was evading its responsibilities. On several occasions they re-affirmed their offer to establish Camps of Discipline but only if the province signified by Order-in-Council that the situation was beyond their control, and before this occurred they would prefer that the province went the full limit of the ordinary criminal law. McNaughton explained federal policy in sending instructions to General Ashton, DOC of Military District 11, and bringing him up to date on federal-provincial correspondence.

> You will observe from this correspondence that it is the purpose of the Dominion Government to insist on the Provincial Government discharging their proper constitutional responsibilities which it is evident they are seeking in certain respects to evade.[44]

For their part, the provincial authorities were fearful that if they insisted upon maximum sentences for vagrancy and other minor offences, the jails, which were a provincial expense, would be filled to overflowing. Attorney-General Sloan expressed such a fear in a telegram to W.A. Gordon on December 15, 1933.

> ...would suggest that to keep arresting discharged men for vagrancy is not solution to problem because term of imprisonment imposed usually short and if long sentences goals would be filled and virtually become relief camps to detriment administration of justice.[45]

Federal officials would later suggest to the B.C. government that they build provincial prison camps to supplement their regular prison facilities.[46] British Columbia considered the idea but rejected it, probably because of the expense and because it did not want to take all of the political flak itself. The pressure to establish Camps of Discipline reached its peak during the winter of 1934 and then declined in June and July—the regular DND camps were usually less populated and quieter during the summer months when inmates would return to the Prairies in search of temporary jobs. For now, the activists among the single unemployed could thank federal-provincial conflict and partisan political jockeying as well as changing public opinion for keeping them out of the prison camps to which all too many government officials would gladly have sent them.

While all of the jockeying was going on, the DND officials were considering various locations for the Camps of Discipline. East Thurlow Island off the British Columbia coast was acquired from B.C. by Ottawa as a Forestry Experimental Area. The negotiations to acquire timber and other rights on the island dragged on for over a year because of the touchiness of British Columbia authorities. The B.C. government did not want to lose revenue from timber or interfere with private timber operations and DND officials were reluctant to inform B.C. politicians, especially Liberals like Premier Pattullo, of what they had in mind for the island. Ottawa did not want to encourage Pattullo to again step up the pressure for federal action which would allow him to "evade his constitutional responsibilities," as McNaughton would put it. They created the impression that they wanted the island merely for forestry experimental purposes and a regular relief camp along the lines of other DND camps. McNaughton hid the real purposes of the negotiations until September 1934. This was revealed in a memorandum summarizing a meeting between McNaughton, Finlayson of the Prime Minister's Office, and Major Turner of the DND on September 13.

> General McNaughton emphasized that he does not wish the question of the possible establishment of a special camp on East Thurlow Island to be discussed in any negotiations with representatives of B.C. but the matter should be settled on the basis of the establishment of a Forest Experimental Station and on the need for providing relief for single homeless unemployed men.[47]

Later in the month, McNaughton decided to reveal to British Columbia authorities what he had in mind for East Thurlow Island, and then they were more cooperative. Premier Duff Pattullo, who often made political capital of criticizing the Bennett government, appeared willing to make arrangements whereby both governments could incarcerate their mutual critics if it became necessary.

General McNaughton, Major Turner, and General E.C. Ashton, DOC of M.D. 11, held a meeting on September 27, 1934, with Premier Pattullo, J.Hart, B.C. Minister of Finance, and E.W. Griffith, Provincial Administrator of Unemployment Relief, at which East Thurlow Island and other matters were discussed. McNaughton pressed the B.C. authorities for a favourable decision on the grounds of the value of a forestry experimental station to British Columbia.

> and, secondly, in order that an isolated camp may be established to which incorrigible personnel eligible for Defence Camps and *nominated by B.C.* may be despatched if circumstances required.[48]

Pattullo, ever mindful of the interests of the taxpayer, was concerned about the loss of $10,000 annual stumpage revenue to the province

> but stated that the remarks of General Mcnaughton placed a different aspect on the matter than had been considered by him previously.[49]

McNaughton also referred to

the secret arrangements which had been concerted to handle the discipline of men creating disturbances in the camps or leaving them and making disturbances elsewhere, should the resources of the civil police not prove adequate.[50]

He stated that the secret arrangements would be invoked only at provincial request and

in view of the general improvement in conditions, it did not seem that any such serious situation as would justify the drastic action was in prospect. The Premier agreed.[51]

Officials from both governments would later encourage each other to take such drastic action in the apparent hope that they themselves would not have to suffer the political consequences.

The federal authorities did ultimately acquire East Thurlow Island and made arrangements for accommodating 250 inmates. However, they did not get around to invoking either the Act or the Order-in-Council and operating a Camp of Discipline there or anywhere else. Part of the reason was that the defiance of constituted authority did not reach the extreme proportions feared by Mcnaughton, at least to the end of 1934, and by then the political situation was such that imprisoning people in Camps of Discipline probably would have caused more upheaval than it prevented.

An important factor was the changing nature and instability of the political situation throughout the country as it related to federal-provincial relations and to manoeuvring among the major political parties. The federal Liberal Party and the CCF had always been extremely critical in Parliament of the "peace, order and good government" clause of the Relief Act of 1933 and would undoubtedly have raised a major political storm, supported in part by the daily press, if the government used the Act to assume dictatorial powers. By 1934 the Conservatives were almost wiped out at the provincial level—they had lost five provincial governments since 1930. Provincial governments, always jealous of their provincial autonomy and now controlled by the opposition, were reluctant to invite Ottawa to assume responsibility for the administration of justice. To do so would be an admission that they were incapable of maintaining law and order.

Only a few government officials knew at the time that the machinery for Camps of Discipline was in place. Several times between early 1933 and mid-1935 government authorities at either the federal or provincial level were recommending the use of such camps to imprison large numbers of people for political reasons. But for the federal-provincial division of power, and the vigilance of those members of the Canadian political community who could be depended upon to vigorously defend liberty, we might have suffered similar oppressive measures to those which were common in several European dictatorships in the same period of history.

Footnotes

1. For a discussion of the B.C. work camps and the change over to the DND camps see Lorne Brown, *The Bennett Government, Political Stability and the Politics of the Unemployment Relief Camps, 1930-35,* unpublished Ph.D. thesis, Queen's University, 1979.
2. Public Archives of Canada (PAC), *McNaughton Papers,* Vol. 58, Brigadier J. Sutherland Brown to Secretary, DND, May 24, 1933.
3. *Ibid.*
4. *Ibid.,* June 1, 1933.
5. *Ibid.,* June 2, 1933.
6. *The Unemployed Worker,* July 5, 1933, p. 2.
7. *McNaughton Papers,* Vol. 58.
8. *Ibid.,* December 12, 1933.
9. *McNaughton Papers,* Vol. 48, 331A, McNaughton memorandum, May 9, 1933. Also see Lorne Brown, "Unemployment Relief camps in Saskatchewan, 1933-36," *Saskatchewan History,* Autumn, 1970, p. 89.
10. Regina *Leader-Post,* May 11, 1933.
11. *Bennett Papers,* File 494777-79, McNaughton to Minister of Defence, October 10, 1933. Also *McNaughton Papers,* File 359 (I).
12. *McNaughton Papers,* File 359 (Vol. I).
13. *Ibid.*
14. House of Commons *Debates*, July 2, 1935. Reprinted in Ronald Liversedge, *Recollections of the On-to-Ottawa Trek,* edited by Victor Hoar (Toronto: McClelland and Stewart Ltd., 1973).
15. Cracked enamelware and crockery were always shunned in work camps as carriers of germs which could cause trench mouth and other ailments of this nature.
16. *McNaughton Papers,* File 359 (Vol. I).
17. *McNaughton Papers,* E.C. Ashton to McNaughton, January 10, 1934.
18. It must be kept in mind that social insurance numbers did not exist, most unemployed did not have driver's licenses, and it was not uncommon for people to carry no personal identification whatsoever during the 1930s.

19. James Gray, *The Winter Years* (Toronto: MacMillan of Canada, 1966), p. 149.
20. *McNaughton Papers,* File 359 (Vol. I).
21. *Ibid.*
22. *Ibid.*
23. *Ibid.*
24. The organized unemployed associations often raised money by holding "tag days" during which members would stand on street corners with tin cans—hence the term "tin canning." These tag days were usually technically illegal but often received widespread public support.
25. *Bennett Papers,* Vol. 1454 (Vol. 800), Roll 395, p. 494519, DOC 13 to CGS, February, 1934.
26. *Bennett Papers,* Vol. 1454 (Vol. 800), Roll 395, McNaughton to Miller, March 2, 1934.
27. *Bennett Papers,* Vol. 1454 (Vol. 800), Roll 395, p. 494246, Bennett to Pattullo, March 2, 1934.
28. *McNaughton Papers,* Vol. 41, 314 (Vol. I), McNaughton to Quartermaster-General, April 3, 1933.
29. *McNaughton Papers,* Vol. 41, McNaughton to Dickson, April 27, 1933.
30. Ottawa *Citizen,* May 29, 1933. Clipping in *McNaughton Papers,* Vol. 41, 314 (Vol. I).
31. The Relief Act of 1933 gave the Governor-in-Council (cabinet) the power when Parliament was not in session "to take all measures as in his discretion may be deemed necessary or advisable to maintain, within the competence of Parliament, peace, order and good government in Canada, ..." It was criticized as giving the federal government the political power to rule by Order-in-Council to a dictatorial extent and, hence, was often referred to as giving the cabinet a "blank cheque" to do as it wished between sessions of Parliament.
32. *Statutes of Canada,* 1932-1933.
33. *McNaughton Papers,* Vol. 41, 314 (Vol. I), McNaughton memorandum, May 31, 1933.
34. *McNaughton Papers,* Vol. 41, McNaughton to Quartermaster-General, June 7, 1933.
35. *McNaughton Papers,* Vol. 41, 314 (Vol. I).
36. *McNaughton Papers,* Vol. 42, 314 (Vol. I), Secret Memorandum from McNaughton to Judge Advocate General, July 1, 1933.
37. *Ibid.*
38. *McNaughton Papers,* Vol. 41, 314 (Vol. I), Rule and Regulation for Camps of Discipline.
39. *McNaughton Papers,* Vol. 41, 314 (Vol. I), W.A. Gordon to S.F. Tolmie, June 19, 1933.
40. *McNaughton Papers,* Vol. 41, 314 (Vol. I), R.H. Poxley to W.A. Gordon, June 21, 1933.
41. *McNaughton Papers,* Vol. 58, H. H. Mathews to McNaughton, July 14, 1933.

42. *McNaughton Papers,* Vol. 58, W.G. Beeman to McNaughton, August 11, 1933.
43. House of Commons *Debates,* 1932, Vol. III, pp. 2658-59, 2638-88, 2716. Also see Chapter II in this book.
44. *McNaughton Papers,* Vol. 58, G.S. Pearson to W.A. Gordon, December 1, 1933.
45. *McNaughton Papers,* Vol. 58, Gordon to Pearson, December 9, 1933.
46. *McNaughton Papers,* Vol. 58, McNaughton to Ashton, December 21, 1933.
47. *McNaughton Papers,* Vol. 58, Gordon Sloan to W.A. Gordon, December 15, 1953.
48. *McNaughton Papers,* Vol. 58, Ashton to McNaughton, December 27, 1933 and McNaughton to Ashton, January 3, 1934.
49. *McNaughton Papers,* Vol. 30, File 99, Memorandum on meeting held in CGS office and attended by McNaughton, Finlayson and Turner on September 13, 1934.
50. *McNaughton Papers,* Vol. 30, File 99, Memorandum on meeting of McNaughton, Turner, Ashton, Pattullo, Hart, Griffith held on September 27, 1934.
51. *Ibid.*

Grading at Relief Project No. 33, Long Branch, Ontario, April 1933. Work was usually done by the most primitive of methods. Long Branch was closed down a few months after it opened because of a bitter strike. (Photo #35370, Public Archives of Canada)

Preparing dinner at DND Relief Project No. 30, Camp Borden, Ontario, May 1933. (Photo #35288, Public Archives of Canada)

Raising truss at the new supply depot, Relief Project No. 39, Val Cartier, Québec, November 1933. (Photo #35440, Public Archives of Canada)

Dinnertime at DND Relief Project No. 103, Duck Mountain, Manitoba, February 1934. (Photo #36591, Public Archives of Canada)

Drilling a 300-ton block at Relief Project No. 122 at the Frank Slide, Alberta, May 1934. (Photo #37107, Public Archives of Canada)

Breaking a foot trail on DND Relief Project No. 56 near Princeton, B.C., January 1935. (Photo #35920, Public Archives of Canada)

CHAPTER V
The Camps as a Political Liability

It was during 1934 that the relief camps became a political issue of considerable significance to a broad cross-section of the public, the press, and the mainstream political parties. These developments coincided with and were a symptom of the growing unpopularity of the Bennett government and the Conservative Party.

Between 1930 and June, 1935, Conservative governments were defeated in Nova Scotia, Manitoba, British Columbia, Saskatchewan, and Ontario. The Conservatives were being systematically wiped out by the electorate across the country. They lost British Columbia in the fall of 1933 and both Saskatchewan and Ontario on June 19, 1934. The last two elections were total routs with the Conservatives being wiped out to the last MLA in Saskatchewan. In B.C. and Saskatchewan the official opposition was formed by the newly founded CCF. The electorates were obviously angry. Ontario and B.C. were now led by Mitch Hepburn and Duff Pattullo respectively—both unorthodox populist Liberals from whom the Bennett regime could expect a great deal of trouble. Saskatchewan was back in the hands of Jimmy Gardiner, an experienced and very partisan Liberal who would not hesitate to attack the federal government with political skill and vigour.

Unemployment had been an issue in all of these provincial campaigns, and especially in B.C. and Ontario where there were many relief camps and the unemployed were well organized both in the camps and in the cities. Both provinces had called for massive public works programmes to relieve unemployment. In both cases the relief camps and the daily allowance of twenty cents a day were attacked by Liberals and other opposition forces as symbolic of the callousness and bankruptcy of the Bennett government in the face of the Depression. Almost all opposition parties in the country—Liberal, CCF and Communist, were by now calling for either abolition of the relief camps and a "work and wages" programme or regular wages and a more democratic regime within the camps. The provincial Conservative losses were interpreted by much of the press, and especially Liberal newspapers, as a repudiation of the economic and social policies of the Bennett government.

It was not just politicians and newspapers criticizing the relief camps by the middle of 1934. Mayors and municipal councillors and private welfare agencies were writing to Bennett and his ministers suggesting that the relief camp system be either radically changed or abolished. The Vancouver Council of Social Agencies wrote to Bennett with a lengthy critique of the camps. They recommended a wage system instead of the twenty cents per day allowance and a system of "welfare committees" elected by camp inmates to handle their grievances.[1] Many church groups and service clubs were making similar suggestions. The idea that something was seriously wrong with the camps had obviously gone beyond labour and political circles.

Even some of Bennett's followers in Parliament were demanding changes. I.D. Cotnam, Conservative M.P. for North Renfrew, Ontario, complained to Bennett in April 1934 that the camps as they were then operated were a political liability to the Conservatives in both provincial and federal politics. Cotnam was particularly worried about the coming Ontario election. "Some action should be taken, at once, with a view to closing the relief camps, or paying the men a reasonable wage."[2] When Bennett did not respond, Cotnam persisted. "The camps are well conducted, but the workingman still continues to regard us as the twenty cents a day party."[3]

Bennett finally moved himself to respond but the patronizing tone and facile explanation he used with his own Members of Parliament indicates that he must have been out of touch with the popular mood.

> You apparently do not understand the purpose of the camps to which you refer. They are just what their name indicates—relief camps; and any man can leave without notice should he desire to take up other employment. We provide the men with food, clothing and shelter, and a small sum per day. We are, in fact, relieving the Province of its obligations with respect to these people. It is too bad that there are those who talk about the

paying of wages. No one suggests that the amount paid is for wages. It is merely a little pocket money for those who are on relief, and we receive letters daily from men who are not able to obtain work who speak in the warmest terms of what is being done for them.[4]

Cotnam was not to be put off. He wrote a stronger letter demanding a wage system and repeating his predictions about the dire political consequences. Bennett closed off his correspondence with Cotnam by declaring that he wanted to hear no more about wages. "I trust you realize that what we are administering is relief and as it is relief there is nothing further that can be said about it."[5]

As representations kept coming in to Bennett about the unpopularity of the twenty cents per day policy he finally developed doubts about the political wisdom of the camps himself but only in private consultations with his officials. He expressed such doubts to McNaughton on May 29, 1934, but was persuaded to continue with the camps on the grounds that without an alternative economic programme to provide work and wages there would be rioting and bloodshed in the cities.[6]

The humiliating Conservative defeats in Saskatchewan and Ontario on June 19, a massive influx of mail against the camps, and the fact that important federal by-elections were coming up in September caused Bennett to again consider closing the relief camps in early July. Again McNaughton and others persuaded him that the camps were absolutely essential to public order.[7] It would have been politically astute at this time to have either closed the camps and replaced them with a meaningful work and wages programme or reformed the relief camp system by democratizing the regulations and paying real wages instead of the twenty cents per day. The government did neither and their popularity continued to decline.

Even if the government was unwilling to pay wages, it could have allowed democratic rights in the relief camps for little or no cost at all. Not only did it refuse to remove the authoritarian regulations but the Bennett government also denied many camp inmates the right to vote in federal elections. Under the Dominion Franchise Act as amended in 1934 certain categories of people who might be away from their home districts on election day were allowed to vote by absentee ballot. Angus MacInnis, CCF M.P. from Vancouver, attempted a further amendment to extend this provision to relief camp inmates.[8] Government members refused to allow the change.

Before the change was disallowed the government was warned by British Columbia M.P. Douglas Neill that the continuing disfranchisement of large numbers of relief camp inmates would be deeply resented and probably lead to trouble. "If this provision does not pass it will leave a sore spot in British Columbia and will be remembered for a long time."[9] Neill also took exception to the way relief camp workers and transient workers generally were viewed by some Members of Parliament.

> Some people think that the word "transient" suggests hoboes, and people of that sort. It is nothing of the kind. It is no crime to have to earn your living away from home and by the methods I have indicated. There is no suggestion that these people are of a low standard because they have to go away to earn their living. Surely they are entitled to a chance to vote.[10]

If anything, Neill was understating the case when he spoke of the bitterness which would result from virtual disfranchisement. The denial of the franchise was looked upon by the single unemployed as another assault on their rights. It was also mentioned frequently from the hustings by opposition politicians, and the right to vote would be one of the demands of the On-to-Ottawa Trek of 1935.

On September 24 the Conservatives lost four out of five federal by-elections in Ontario to the Liberals. One seat, Frontenac-Addington, had never been Liberal before, and another, York North, had nearly always been a Conservative seat. The Conservatives retained only one riding and there they suffered a sharply reduced majority; the CCF picked up nearly 4000 votes and split the opposition. The by-election results, like the earlier provincial elections, were interpreted by the opposition and much of the press as additional proof that the Bennett government was thoroughly discredited. The Regina *Leader-Post* was typical of Liberal newspaper reaction by interpreting the results as meaning that Canadians wanted the Bennett government out of office as quickly as possible.

> Its policies are not acceptable to the Canadian people. Every major action of the Government is in defiance of the wishes of the Canadian people.[11]

The *Leader-Post* was probably fairly close to being correct, as the election results a year later would show. In fact, the results would show that more Canadians than ever before had rejected both the Conservative and Liberal parties. By September 1934 the tide had turned against both the relief camp system and the Bennett government in general.

By now the more perceptive Conservatives knew their party was in serious trouble. But few of these had the ear of Bennett and the federal cabinet. H.H. Stevens, minister of trade and commerce, had been agitating within the party for a broad range of economic and social reforms. Stevens had previously headed up the Price Spreads Commission which had exposed labour and pricing abuses in the retail trade and the clothing industry. For his efforts Stevens was attacked by the owners of Eaton's, Simpson's, and other corporate giants, with the result that Stevens was isolated within the cabinet and forced to resign. Unfortunately for the party and the country, Stevens and his followers had little influence over the Bennett cabinet. He would soon split from the Conservative Party altogether and run his own Reconstruction Party in the election of 1935.

Immediately after the September by-election defeats a number of Conservative M.P.'s. would begin privately agitating for changes in the administration of the relief camps and especially for a wage system, however modest, to replace the twenty cents per diem allowance. The Bennett cabinet stuck to the relief strategy they had pursued for four years and refused to budge. Meanwhile, the relief camps were filling up for the winter and the Relief Camp Workers' Union was preparing a major offensive to obtain work and wages either within a drastically reformed camp system or outside the camps altogether.

The extent to which the workers of the DND camps in British Columbia were becoming organized is indicated by the fact that the RCWU held a conference of representatives from throughout the province in August 1934. [12] This conference planned a campaign for the coming months around a specific programme which demanded work and wages, that relief camp workers be covered by workers' compensation, an end to blacklisting, an end to military control of the camps, and recognition of camp committees. The programme also demanded a minimum wage of forty cents per hour in the camps. [13]

By this time, Arthur (Slim) Evans was working as a full-time paid organizer for the Workers' Unity League in British Columbia. His main assignment was to organize the RCWU into a more effective union. Evans brought to the task a wealth of experience. Though born in Toronto in 1888, he had lived most of his adult life in the mining and resource regions of the American and Canadian West. Evans had also been an activist in labour struggles all his life. He did time in prison for his activities in an IWW Free Speech fight in Kansas City in 1912. Evans was wounded at the time of the infamous Ludlow Massacre in 1913 when miners and their families were gunned down by the militia during a miners' strike against the Rockefeller interests in Ludlow, Colorado. Evans later organized for the One Big Union in the coal fields of Drumheller, Alberta, during the 1920s and was one of the scores of OBU activists imprisoned during these years of conflict. He would go to prison again for leading a coal miners' strike in Princeton, B.C., in 1933. His most recent job had been as B.C. organizer of the National Unemployed Workers' Association.

Evans was a superb organizer and leader. He was tough, shrewd, audacious, politically sophisticated, and totally dedicated. He was the sort of person around whom legends grow and was generally well liked and respected by those with whom he worked, even when they did not agree with his political opinions or his particular strategy. He inspired confidence in people.

Evans was assisted by scores of volunteer activists who worked without pay as proselytizers and organizers for the RCWU. Most of them were extremely dedicated and possessed a great deal of political skill. They relied upon the "bush committees" in the camps and could depend upon support in the cities from the organized unemployed, trade unions, and leftist sympathizers. By December 1934 the RCWU and their allies were prepared for the biggest offensive yet in support of their demands.

The offensive began on December 7 when a large delegation representing associations of the unemployed, both married and single, from throughout the province met with Premier Pattullo and his cabinet in Victoria. The delegation was backed up by a demonstration of about 500 unemployed and presented a petition signed by 30,665 people and endorsed by sixty-five associations. [14] In addition to the relief camp demands agreed upon in August there were demands on behalf of the urban unemployed which included a fifty per cent increase in relief allowances, uniform rates throughout the province, and a food allowance of at least forty-five cents daily for the single unemployed in urban areas. The entire action was well planned and well executed with a broad support base.

The premier expressed sympathy for the unemployed but insisted the province could afford no additional costs and the problem would have to be solved by the federal government. "Premier Pattullo declared emphatically that the problem was national but that conditions would ultimately force its solution. He predicted that Canada would have to embark upon a large public works programme to give employment to its citizens and his government was working consistently towards this end."[15]

On the same day a separate delegation representing the RCWU met with Pattullo, his labour minister, and two officers from the DND headquarters to press the specific demands of the relief camp inmates. They were given no satisfaction and, in fact, Colonel Greer of the DND denied that a "blacklist" existed.[16] According to General McNaughton

> the outcome of the interview was firm statement that none of their demands could be met in any way, and there was nothing stated that could in any way be construed into promising them that any of their demands were acceded to.[17]

The demonstrations and meetings in Victoria drew considerable editorial comment in the British Columbia press. Much of the comment was sympathetic to the organized unemployed and some of it was indicative of the extent to which "mainstream" opinion had changed since 1932 in that it not only expressed sympathy for the plight of the unemployed but also indicated a willingness to endorse mass protests as a necessary and healthy occurrence. No longer untypical was an editorial in the Vancouver *Daily Province.*

> The organization of relief is so complete now, after some years' experience, that we hear few objections to it, few revolts against it. That may be very pleasing for the authorities administering it. But it is not a condition to be accepted complacently. Ructions in relief camps, walkouts, committees of unemployed, are evidence of virility and independence that should be accepted with gladness and treated with patience, not frowned upon and suppressed.[18]

This type of outlook was to become more widespread among journalists and a broad cross-section of opposition politicians and the public in the months ahead.

On the day of the Victoria demonstration widespread strikes and, in some instances, walkouts began in DND camps scattered throughout the province. Within a few days several hundred men had been expelled from the camps for refusal to work and several hundred more had left in sympathy. They began making their way towards Vancouver where they would be joined in mass demonstrations by the unemployed. There were also demonstrations in smaller cities throughout the province.

Events began escalating quickly and the extent and militancy of the protest probably caught the authorities off guard. On December

10 between fifty and 100 local unemployed men and some of their wives occupied the relief offices in Nanaimo and imprisoned two government relief officials inside the buildings.[19] This action had to do with local grievances of the Nanaimo unemployed. The occupation ended on December 12 when the police broke down the door with sledgehammers and dispersed the demonstrators. The only injury reported was the case of one man cut by flying glass.

On December 11 several hundred relief camp strikers marched into Vancouver and demonstrated before Police Headquarters demanding food and lodging.[20] Police Chief John Cameron, after a telephone conversation with the Attorney-General at Victoria, issued "script" which would provide the men with food and lodging at the Salvation Army and similar establishments for one week "pending negotiations as to the return of the strikers to their camps."[21] The Vancouver *Daily Province* described the men as well organized and orderly. The spokesman for the demonstrators warned that 600 more were expected to reach Vancouver from the camps in a few days and the provincial police reported that several more camps had walked out.

By December 13 there were at least 500 striking relief camp workers in Vancouver. Their spokesmen visited the offices of the *Daily Province* where they claimed that 4000 men in twenty relief camps would strike unless blacklisting was ended.[22] They also emphasized their demands for a wage system and the right to vote in federal elections.

Federal, provincial and municipal authorities were obviously alarmed at the magnitude of the RCWU offensive but disagreed on how to deal with it. The federal government maintained a hard line no compromise position. They refused to even acknowledge that blacklisting existed and would offer no concessions on the other demands. They also pressed municipal and provincial officials to offer no relief in the cities. The federal strategy was to starve the relief camp strikers back into the camps. They would re-admit all strikers but those they considered ringleaders and agitators.

Pattullo's cabinet disagreed among themselves on how to handle the situation—fluctuating between a hard line and compromise. They handled the crises as they erupted on an almost day-to-day basis with no consistent policy. Attorney-General Sloan authorized Police Chief Cameron to issue script to alleviate an immediate crisis and stall for time. On December 15, four days after authorizing the original script, Cameron and provincial officials issued a statement to the effect that no further script would be issued except to men who applied for reinstatement to the camps and to tide them over until their applications were processed. And there would be no further aid to anyone leaving the camps after December 15.[23] On December 16 Cameron returned to Vancouver from the Victoria meeting to discover 250 men besieging the police station for aid. They had read about the new arrangements in the Saturday papers and were quick to take advantage of them. As the Employment Service of Canada was closed for the weekend the Chief had little choice but to issue script without first compelling the men to apply for reinstatement. They had out-manoeuvred the authorities, at least temporarily, and more men were en route to Vancouver, so it would be difficult to determine whether men had left the camps before or after December 15. And very few of those already in Vancouver applied for reinstatement in the camps.

DND officials put more pressure on the provincial authorities. They agreed to take a hard line about denying relief to men leaving or expelled from the camps and Labour Minister Pearson even provided the DND with a written assurance to this effect.[24] The result was a public statement from the provincial government on December 17 to the effect that such relief would be denied.[25] That same day the RCWU sent an open letter to Premier Pattullo and "all government and relief officials" repudiating the conditions for returning to the camps and refusing to return while the blacklist remained in force.

> We hereby instruct our strike committee to inform you of our stand and declare ourselves for immediate and complete abolition of the blacklist system as the only condition under which we will return to the camps.[26]

Meanwhile, unrest in the camps was reported by the press to be fairly general and more walkouts were feared.

> The situation in the camps east of here is somewhat tense. There have been rumours of a general strike in all camps, and already a number of camps have had trouble. B.C. police officers are patrolling the camps at the present time.[27]

Without a compromise, tension was likely to increase rather than lessen. The Vancouver municipal authorities and business community were worried that street demonstrations and the possibility of violence would have a negative effect on business during the Christmas shopping season. They preferred at least a temporary compromise to cool out the situation. With this in mind, Mayor Louis D. Taylor of Vancouver telephoned Premier Pattullo on December 18 to protest the provincial decision to deny further relief to the former relief camp inmates who were now estimated to number about 700 in the city. The mayor informed the newspapers of his protest and consultation with Pattullo and it became a major news story.

> In his conversation with Premier Pattullo, the Mayor observed that public opinion will be opposed to cutting the men adrift at the Christmas season. He pointed out that any street disturbance at present would injure the Christmas trade. The Mayor urged that the governments continue providing for the men until Christmas is over, on the understanding that any men who leave camp from now on will not be given aid. The Premier explained that the Department of Defence representatives in Victoria have conferred with Hon. Gordon Sloan and Hon. G.S. Pearson and demand a "showdown." They fear that continuation of relief to men in town would lead to a general desertion of the camps. [28]

It was now clear to the organized unemployed and the public that the federal and provincial governments were willing to risk a "showdown" with the relief strikers but that the city wished to avoid a confrontation if at all possible.

On the day that Mayor Taylor issued his statement the single unemployed demonstrated in front of the Vancouver provincial relief office and then marched to the police station to demand assistance. The script issued on December 11 had run out the day before and a confrontation now seemed probable. At this stage a newly formed private citizens' group stepped into the picture. They met the strikers at the police station and provided tickets for food and lodging. According to a representative of the citizens' group, "We could not see the men going hungry. We have provided for temporary assistance until some arrangement can be made by government authorities to meet the situation." [29]

This new group was to play a crucial role in the next two weeks. Many members of the group had contacts with the Vancouver Council of Social Agencies and other middle-class circles. They were additional proof that Mayor Taylor had sensed public opinion quite correctly. The group played a dual role in that they provided temporary sustenance to many of the relief camp strikers and acted as mediators between the strikers and the three levels of government. One of their first acts was to try to persuade federal and provincial officials to make concessions at a "private, informal conference" with various voluntary welfare associations on December 19 in Vancouver. The two levels of government held firm: there would be no relief until the men applied for re-admission to the camps.

On the same day an editorial entitled "An Intolerable Situation" in the Vancouver *Daily Province* was highly critical of both federal and provincial officials and claimed that the people and municipal government of Vancouver were being made "scapegoats" by the irresponsible attitude of the higher levels of government. The editorial took no direct stand on the specific grievances of the single unemployed and also asserted that discipline must be maintained in the camps but also cast doubt on the value of the relief camps as an answer to the unemployment problem.

> There could be no tolerable maintenance of such camps unless some sort of discipline were enforced. Equally we have no doubt that there are grievances among the men in the camps—for it is grievance enough that they are there at all and that their country and their fellow citizens can find no better remedy for the disease of unemployment. [30]

The strongest part of the editorial was a vociferous protest against what the *Daily Province* saw as a dangerous situation caused by federal and provincial politicians.

> We should be extremely loathe to aggravate by a single unconsidered word an unhappy situation between the men of the camps and the authorities. But there is no sense in the attitude of the authorities as it affects this community. That attitude apparently is that 700 men homeless in the streets of Vancouver, are to be starved into submission. Premier Pattullo is reported as saying, in reply to the proper protests of Mayor Taylor, that the Department of Defence "wants a showdown," and takes the view that giving relief to the men who have quit the camps would lead to a general desertion of the camps. The logic of this is that the men are to be allowed to starve to death—unless they prefer to riot—in the streets of Vancouver—and that is just outrageous nonsense. It is not for us to tell the Dominion and Provincial authorities what they ought to do to settle their trouble, but it is decidedly our business to tell them that they are not settling it, but are running away from it, when they attempt to shoulder it off upon the people of this city. [31]

The *Daily Province* was probably expressing the fears of many influential Vancouverites when they referred to the possibility of riots if the senior levels of government did not alter their strategy towards the single unemployed. It was likely this factor, more than anything else, which caused those professional and business people for whom Mayor Taylor was the spokesman to demand a compromise solution. It was this which gave the organized unemployed more bargaining power in dealing with senior governments.

By December 20 the informal citizens group had constituted itself as the "Citizens Committee" and was recognized as a special committee of the Vancouver Council of Social Agencies. It had become the generally recognized unofficial mediator of the dispute and its representatives met with federal and provincial officials in the early afternoon of December 20 in an attempt to gain concessions on the blacklisting problem. Having failed, they then proceeded to 52-½ Cordoba Street where a mass meeting sponsored by the RCWU was in progress. They were allowed to address the meeting and proposed that the men seek reinstatement in the camps and allow the Citizens' Committee to carry on negotiations for abolition of the blacklist. It was pointed out that relief from private sources was running out and that there was no guarantee of relief for the next day.

The single unemployed decided to hold firm and to attempt to enlarge the struggle. The meeting unanimously turned down the proposal and voted in favour of a general strike in the camps and a march on Vancouver. Mr. H. MacDonald and Mr. F.R. Forbes, members of the strikers' publicity committee, declared that the men were not willing to go back to the camp without their leaders.

> If we follow the suggestion of government officials and return to camp it means that our leaders will be blacklisted and forced to roam the streets of Vancouver without food or shelter.[32]

The problem of blacklisting was to be an issue on which the RCWU and their supporters held firm until they gained concessions.

The Citizens' Committee continued trying to mediate between the RCWU and the authorities. Meanwhile, various member agencies of the Council of Social Agencies continued to supply relief to at least some of the relief camp strikers; others managed to get along for the next few days with assistance from individual sympathizers and donations from trade unions and political groups like the Communist Party and the CCF.

On December 21 Premier Pattullo, who had previously let his ministers do the talking in public, made his first major public statement on the crisis since the offensive began on December 7. It came in the form of a letter to the editor of the Vancouver *Daily Province*. He claimed that Vancouver was not being made the "scapegoat" and that the province was doing all that was possible for the single unemployed. Pattullo again called for a massive federal programme of public works as an alternative to the camps and insisted that until that was achieved the men return to the camps. The trouble was blamed on unreasonable agitators. This was to be Pattullo's public stance in the coming months—the federal government should provide work and wages instead of camps, but, meanwhile, the province could do nothing and the single unemployed should behave themselves.

The Citizens' Committee attempted a new strategy. They recommended that the men return in exchange for a promise that the federal government would establish an independent commission of enquiry into the relief camp system. Regarding the immediate issue of blacklisting the Committee recommended that, if the DND would not end the blacklist, those blacklisted be maintained by the province pending the report of the suggested commission of enquiry.

The temporary solution proposed by the Citizens' Committee began to look attractive to the RCWU. By December 22 (the Saturday before Christmas) the full scale general strike and the march on Vancouver which had been called for by the mass meeting of December 20 had not materialized. The RCWU had hoped that several thousand would walk out and descend upon Vancouver but by December 22 there were about 1000 strikers in the city. They had apparently over-estimated the extent of the unrest and their own strength and efficiency as an organization. Other factors included stormy weather in parts of the province which made travelling difficult and the prospect of staying in the camps less unappealing. Camp inmates were not required to work in stormy or extremely cold weather and they were due for three days rest anyway—Sunday, Christmas and Boxing Day.

Vancouver authorities were given a reprieve, but the problem remained: what to do with the 1000 who were still holding firm in the city and what would happen in the camps immediately after Christmas. The problem of sustenance was again temporarily overcome on December 24 when Vancouver City Council agreed to provide relief for Christmas Day and Boxing Day. Many trade unionists and political sympathizers also invited single unemployed people to spend Christmas Day at their homes.

Local politicians and voluntary associations now mounted a tremendous pressure campaign to convince the Bennett government to agree to an independent commission of enquiry or a conciliation board and to either abolish blacklisting or compromise on the issue. This campaign crossed all party lines as revealed by a telegram sent to the prime minister signed by all Vancouver MP's and MLA's, eight in number and including Liberals, Conservatives and CCF. Their message was very forceful and recommended immediate action to avert serious trouble.

> The following federal and provincial members of parliament for greater Vancouver wish to bring to your immediate attention the exceedingly urgent situation now existing here with regard to single, homeless men who have left or have been compelled to leave national defence camps. We unanimously recommend first establishment of independent commission of investigation and secondly abolition of the alleged discriminatory blacklist. Recommend immediate provision by Federal Government for the maintenance and sustenance for these men until a full and impartial investigation is held into the entire situation. Otherwise situation here may develop very grave and serious aspects. [33]

On the same day Mayor Taylor sent a telegram to Bennett demanding an impartial enquiry. On December 26 Premier Pattullo got into the act with a telegram to Bennett. He took a position which was becoming his stock-in-trade—simultaneously recommending concessions and more political repression.

> Citizens very alarmed at situation in Vancouver. Vancouver City has for forty-eight hours been feeding men who have left camps. Representations made majority of men will go back to camp if men who have refused re-admission be taken care of by same authority. The incorrigibles are pariahs and keeping reasonably minded in constant agitation. Situation at present drifting and somebody likely to get hurt. I suggest that those unamenable to authority must be disciplined and policy must be adopted of providing work. Meantime I re-suggest that impartial tribunal be set up to consider camp situation. [34]

Pattullo followed this up on December 27 with a further telegram to Bennett emphasizing the gravity of the situation and explicitly warning that people might be killed.

> This situation should be righted immediately before serious consequences with probable loss of life. [35]

He again recommended an impartial tribunal and proposed a segregated camp for blacklisted men. Of all the politicians involved, Pattullo's reasoning was perhaps the most difficult to understand. On the one hand, he argued for an end to the camps, and work and wages so long as it was at federal expense, and an impartial

96

investigation. On the other hand, so long as he did not have to accept responsibility for it, Pattullo urged the federal government to lock up those very leaders of the unemployed who were also agitating for a work and wages programme. Pattullo did not explain why—with blacklisting recognized as such a crucial issue to the organized unemployed—he thought they themselves and the public would be likely to stand for the imprisonment of these blacklisted leaders.

The DND and the federal government were in no mood for compromise. DND officials were fully prepared to implement Pattullo's advice: to imprison the agitators if the Bennett cabinet and the province gave the green light. On December 28 McNaughton summed up the British Columbia situation in a memorandum to the prime minister, the minister of defence, and the minister and deputy minister of labour. He suggested that the response of the federal authorities should be the same as that during previous crises. Men who had been expelled from the camps should be re-instated by military authorities "provided there is, in their opinion, a reasonable probability of the men properly behaving in future."[36] In other words, the blacklist would be continued.

In respect to the possibility of violence or disorder McNaughton drew the attention of the ministers to previous offers to B.C. of military intervention and prison camps upon formal request.[37] The DND was now fully prepared to begin operating such camps.

> All preliminary arrangements in respect to Camps of Discipline have been made and all necessary instructions and regulations and drafts of Orders-in-Council are in the hands of all D.O.C.'s ready for use.[38]

Bennett's reply to Pattullo made no mention of Camps of Discipline or segregated camps. Apparently he either considered them unwise or calculated that Pattullo would never pass the necessary provincial Order-in-Council and accept joint responsibility for an escalation of the political repression. But the prime minister refused any concessions whatsoever. He contended that conditions in the camps were perfectly alright and that the only ones dissatisfied were a handful of agitators and people who had been "duped" by them. Since there was already, in Bennett's view, a very satisfactory system of hearing grievances, the establishment of an independent commission would merely be an unnecessary concession to RCWU agitators.[39] Pattullo and his ministers were urged to do more to inform the public about the virtues of the relief camp system.

While the Bennett and Pattullo governments were carrying on their private debate, the Citizens' Committee and others in Vancouver continued their attempts to arrive at a compromise solution to the immediate crisis. A series of meetings involving members of City Council and the Vancouver Council of Social Agencies, local MLA's and M.P.'s and representatives of the RCWU arrived at a solution which they thought might, with a few amendments, be acceptable to the single unemployed who would have to vote on it at a mass meeting. Under the terms of the proposed plan the single unemployed would be given one week's relief by the city and the province providing they applied for re-instatement in the camps by December 31. Those who accepted would be returned to the camps as soon as possible and meanwhile would continue to receive relief. Single unemployed from outside British Columbia could, as an alternative, be given transportation to their last place of domicile. Those people believed to be blacklisted would also apply for re-instatement and "may be returned to the camp at the discretion of the defence department."[40] It was left unclear what would happen to them or who would support them if they were not re-instated. The provincial government promised to keep pressing Ottawa for an independent enquiry commission on the camps in general and the specific problem of blacklisting.

Two important details remained to be worked out to make the proposed agreement acceptable to the rank and file of the single unemployed. One involved a federal agreement to establish an independent commission; the other concerned what would become of the men who were not accepted back into the camps. While the tentative agreement had not been formally accepted by the RCWU or a mass meeting of the strikers, pending clarification of these two issues, both the single unemployed and the local authorities began operating on the assumption that an agreement would soon be reached. On Friday evening, December 28, 843 men were granted one week's relief on condition that they apply on Monday for re-instatement in the camps.

Over the weekend more pressure was brought to bear on Prime Minister Bennett to at least make the minor concession of an independent commission so the agreement could be concluded. On December 29 a meeting of local politicians was held in Vancouver for the sole purpose of sending a telegram to Bennett appealing for a change in policy. They sent the following telegram:

> On evidence as has been presented to us we are of opinion that there are at least in some camps conditions which constitute

sufficient cause for a thorough investigation. And whereas we are informed that British Columbia government has asked federal government to appoint a tribunal we respectfully urge the appointment of an independent commission to investigate first general conditions obtaining in camps which appear to cause dissatisfaction and secondly circumstances surrounding expulsion of men from camps for other than offences against the criminal or civil codes of Canada or provincial statutes. [41]

The telegram was signed by three M.P.'s, eight MLA's, ten Vancouver aldermen, and J.A.T. Folk for the Vancouver Council of Social Agencies. Premier Pattullo sent his own telegram on the same day reiterating his request for an independent commission of enquiry.

Bennett's response to these requests came in the form of a telegram to Pattullo in which he did not even acknowledge the renewed calls for an independent commission.

Your wire twenty-ninth December. Cordially invite you or any of your Ministers to visit any camp maintained by Defence Department in British Columbia or elsewhere and to express your opinion of them. All facilities will be given by District Officer Commanding. [42]

This was part of Bennett's strategy, which he was to develop further in the next few months, of attempting to co-opt Pattullo and his government into making common cause with the federal government in a defence of the relief camp system before the public. Bennett sensed that the premier would not go beyond proposing alternatives to the camp system and actually take the part of the men against the camp authorities. It would go against the grain of the man. But Pattullo, whatever he might think in private, was too shrewd a politician to be drawn in on the side of an increasingly discredited and unpopular federal government. By this time any politician who defended the camps did so at the risk of his political future.

It became apparent by December 30 that if the immediate crisis was to be overcome without a nasty and perhaps violent clash between the single unemployed and the authorities, the solution would have to be found in Vancouver and Victoria with little help from the Bennett government. Over the next few days a series of meetings and consultations worked out a compromise agreement acceptable to the provincial and municipal authorities and the RCWU and their supporters. The final agreement, accepted by a mass meeting of strikers on January 2, was a slight refinement of the proposed agreement of December 28. The strikers applied for re-admission to the camps and were maintained by the province and City of Vancouver while their applications were processed. The province agreed to continue pressuring the Bennett government for an independent tribunal to investigate the camps in general and blacklisting in particular. While the investigation was taking place (assuming such a tribunal was appointed) those blacklisted and not accepted by the DND for re-instatement would be maintained by the province in Vancouver.

The agreement involved considerable compromise by the single unemployed and some by the province. The strikers agreed to return to the camps without any solid guarantee that an independent commission would be appointed. And they had won none of their other demands so that most of the grievances which had led to the walkout in the first place remained. The province, at least by implication, had agreed to provide relief indefinitely to those RCWU activists whom the DND had blacklisted from the camps. They had thus gone back on their previous agreement with the DND to refuse relief to anyone expelled from the camps. The federal government had conceded nothing, and, as events would illustrate over the next few months, appears to have learned little from a month of almost continuous crises.

The single unemployed began registering for and returning to the camps on January 3. Within a couple of weeks all had returned except for about 100 whom the DND had rejected and slightly more than 100 others whom they were still considering. These people remained in Vancouver and were provided relief by the provincial government.

The British Columbia relief camps returned to a state of relative calm in the dead of winter. Both the authorities and the public would soon realize that it was the calm before the storm.

Footnotes

1. Public Archives of Canada (PAC), *Bennett Papers*, File No. 495167, McNelly to Bennett, April 18, 1934.
2. *Ibid.*, File No. 494549, Cotnam to Bennett, April 27, 1934.
3. *Ibid.*, File No. 494555, Cotnam to Bennett, May 9, 1934.
4. *Ibid.*, File No. 494557, Bennett to Cotnam, May 14, 1934.
5. *Ibid.*, Bennett to Cotnam, May 25, 1934.

6. McNaughton memorandum, May 30, 1934, quoted in James Eayrs, *In Defence of Canada*, Vol. I (Toronto: University of Toronto Press, 1964), p. 132.
7. James Eayrs, *op. cit.*, pp. 131, 132, and John Swettenham, *McNaughton*, Vol. I (Toronto: The Ryerson Press, 1968), pp. 227-278.
8. House of Commons *Debates*, June 29, 1934, p. 4506, Relief camp residents had been allowed to vote in provincial elections in B.C., Saskatchewan and Ontario in 1933 and 1934, though in Ontario there were some residency changes and movement of camp personnel made it more difficult. The fact that they were allowed to vote provincially but denied the franchise federally was an additional sore point.
9. House of Commons *Debates*, June 20, 1934, p. 4525.
10. *Ibid.*
11. Regina *Leader-Post*, "Through With Mr. Bennett," September 25, 1934.
12. Gladys Stone, "The Regina Riot: 1935," unpublished M.A. thesis, University of Saskatchewan, 1967, p. 9.
13. *Bennett Papers*, File No. 495451, *op. cit.* In many parts of the country fifty cents per hour was the going wage for common labour in 1934, particularly in those few instances where common labour was unionized.
14. Vancouver *Daily Province*, December 7, 1934, p. 18.
15. *Ibid.*
16. PAC, *McNaughton Papers*, File 359, Vol. 2, Memorandum of December 28, 1934, "Situation in British Columbia in respect to congestion of single homeless men in Vancouver discharged or leaving relief camps." Hereinafter cited as McNaughton Memorandum, December 28, 1934.
17. *Ibid.*
18. Vancouver *Daily Province*, December 8, 1934, p. 6.
19. *Ibid.*, December 11, 1934, p. 1.
20. *Ibid.*, December 12, 1934, p. 1, and McNaughton Memorandum, December 28, 1934.
21. *Ibid.*, December 12, 1934, p. 1.
22. *Ibid.*, December 13, 1934, p. 1.
23. *Ibid.*, December 15, 1934.
24. McNaughton Memorandum, *op. cit.*, December 28, 1934.
25. *Ibid.*, *Daily Province*, December 17, 1934, p. 1.
26. *Ibid.*, December 18, 1934, p. 5.
27. *Ibid.*, December 17, 1934, p. 1.
28. *Ibid.*, December 18, 1934, p. 8.
29. *Ibid.*, December 19, 1934, p. 1.
30. *Ibid.*, p. 6.
31. *Ibid.*
32. *Ibid.*, December 20, 1934.
33. *Bennett Papers*, File No. 495502, MacInnis, *et. al.*, to Bennett, December 24, 1934.
34. *Ibid.*, File No. 495513-14, Pattullo to Bennett, December 26, 1934.
35. *Ibid.*, File No. 495516-18, Pattullo to Bennett, December 27, 1934.

36. McNaughton Memorandum, *op. cit.*, December 28, 1934.
37. *Ibid.* The offers had been made on February 25, 1934, and December 19, 1933.
38. *Ibid.*
39. *Bennett Papers, op. cit.,* Bennett to Pattullo, December 28, 1934.
40. Vancouver *Daily Province,* December 29, 1934, p. 2.
41. *Bennett Papers,* File No. 495541, Ian Mackenzie, *et. al.,* to Bennett, December 29, 1934.
42. *Bennett Papers,* File No. 495544, Bennett to Pattullo, December 29, 1934.

CHAPTER VI

Mass Walkout in British Columbia and Stalemate in Vancouver

The Relief Camp workers' Union and local politicians continued to press the federal government for concessions and a public inquiry during January and February 1935. The insensitivity of the federal authorities to this pressure was to set the stage for an escalation of the conflict between the organized unemployed and all levels of government.

Despite the frequency and persistence of demands for changes, or at the very least an inquiry, Bennett's ministers refused to budge. They continued to refuse despite warnings from military officials in British Columbia. Major-General E.C. Ashton, DOC of MD 11, made a lengthy report to National Defence headquarters in which he emphasized that public opinion was with the single unemployed and out of sympathy with the relief camp system. Ashton pleaded for action: "It certainly appears to me advisable that some action to restore public confidence in the same system is needed." [1]

Ashton's advice went unheeded, and, not surprisingly, the level of unrest in the relief camps increased. There were numerous reports of strikes and outbreaks. The most severe outbreak occurred at Deep Bay relief camp on February 9 when the inmates destroyed their bedding, smashed windows, doors, and wash basins, and assaulted the camp foremen. Thirteen men were arrested and ten received prison sentences. [2] The outbreaks of February do not appear to have been part of a coordinated strategy by the RCWU. These disturbances had more the mark of spontaneity and were probably a sign that unrest was reaching new heights.

While the unrest was building the RCWU were attempting to strengthen their organization and prepare a new offensive. General McNaughton received intelligence reports to the effect that the B.C. and Alberta relief camp workers had amalgamated their organizations and were probably planning a major action in conjunction with other relief recipients. "It is believed that a mass strike of camp workers and the relief recipients is to be called April 1, 1935."[3]

Most well informed people in British Columbia were aware that a new explosion was inevitable unless something was done to alleviate the unrest. Provincial and municipal officials and private citizens and groups increased the pressure on Bennett. This time, the Vancouver Board of Trade entered the picture by appointing a committee to monitor the situation and recommend steps to avoid a repetition of the mass walkout of the previous December. The Board of Trade committee amalgamated with the Citizens' Committee which had operated under the auspices of the Vancouver Council of Social Agencies to help negotiate an end to the December strike. This new creation became known as the Joint Citizens' Committee and operated under the chairmanship of Mr. J.W. Deb Farris.

Farris sent a telegram to Prime Minister Bennett on February 25, 1935, pointing out that the relief camp workers had returned to the camps in January only after the B.C. government, Vancouver City Council, and the Citizens' Committee had promised to continue pressing Ottawa for an independent inquiry. There was still no sign of a commission of inquiry and the Joint Citizens' Committee was becoming concerned.

> Joint Committee has met on three occasions, is in receipt of information as to developments in camp situation and believe only a matter of time before further trouble on more serious basis will develop. In interests of peace and order and to prevent destruction of property in city and interference with business joint committee hopes that you authorize official investigation of the camp situation by a citizens' committee.[4]

Bennett's reply to Farris was to reiterate his opposition to an independent inquiry and suggest that British Columbia and Vancouver municipal politicians visit the camps themselves and report to the public. It was a continuation of the federal strategy of attempting to manoeuvre local politicians into defending the relief camp system or at least making common cause with the federal government against the RCWU.

While politicians and private citizens in Vancouver attempted to move what appeared to be an unmovable federal government, the RCWU proceeded with plans for a general strike of relief camp workers throughout British Columbia and western Alberta. On March 15, 1935, the RCWU met in Kamloops with delegates from British Columbia and a few from Alberta. Arthur (Slim) Evans, who was later to become the main leader of the On-to-Ottawa Trek, attended on behalf of the Workers' Unity League.[5]

The Kamloops conference agreed to attempt a mass walkout from as many camps as possible on April 4. Those from the British Columbia camps would make their way to Vancouver and a smaller number from some of the Alberta camps would travel to Calgary. The delegates made plans for support groups in the various towns en route and for labour support, including sympathy strikes where possible, from WUL affiliates and other sympathetic unions.

The delegates at Kamloops also agreed that the mass strike of April 4 be based around seven demands to the federal government. The demands were:

> 1. That work and wages be instituted at the minimum wage of 50 cents per hour for unskilled workers and trade union rates for skilled workers on the basis of a six-hour day, five day week, with a minimum of twenty work days per month.
> 2. That all workers working in camps be covered by the Compensation Act and that adequate first aid supplies be carried on the job at all times.
> 3. That the National Defence and all military control of the camps with the system of blacklisting where men are cut off from all means of livelihood, be abolished.
> 4. That democratically elected committees be recognized in every camp.
> 5. That there be instituted a system of non-contributory unemployment insurance based on the Workers' Bill of Social and Unemployment Insurance.
> 6. That all workers be given their democratic right to vote.
> 7. That Section 98 of the Criminal Code, Sections 41 and 42 of the Immigration Act, vagrancy laws and all anti-working class laws be repealed.[6]

The list of demands went beyond the immediate grievances of the men in the camps and it appears obvious that the RCWU did not believe that one major strike could wrest such concessions from the Bennett government. Even those demands relating directly to the camps would, if granted, drastically alter the existing relief camp system and be a major accomplishment. It seems probable that the RCWU viewed the demands relating to the camps as a bargaining position which might lead to significant concessions. The demands relating to unemployment insurance and amendments to the Criminal Code and the Immigration Act were probably an attempt to build a broader base and to publicize the general political programme of the Workers' Unity League. While it was highly unlikely that they would be granted by the Conservative government, these demands enjoyed considerable support from the public. Most trade unions, including many of the more conservative ones, supported them. And both the Liberal Party and the CCF as well as the entire civil liberties movement were committed to the repeal of Section 98 of the Criminal Code. These demands were useful for building political alliances and commendable as a longer run aim, but those relating directly to the camps stood a better chance of being at least partially granted. As the agitation developed around the walkout the immediate demands were given the most prominence.

Even before the Kamloops conference turmoil had again become general in the camps. On March 16 General Ashton informed General Mcnaughton that militant protests were occurring constantly in many of the camps and the administrators in some camps were beginning to "break" under the strain.[7]

As the situation built up towards the walkout the reaction of the authorities was very similar to that of December 1934 in that the federal government was unwilling to take positive action and provincial officials urged positive action providing it was totally at federal expense. Ashton met with Premier Pattullo and Attorney-General Sloan to discuss the problems of maintaining order during the expected walkout. Not surprisingly, Ashton found the two politicians "considerably alarmed" at the situation. Pattullo and Sloan both knew that by now public opinion was overwhelmingly with the single unemployed and, in the event of a confrontation, therefore, they did not wish to appear to be siding with the federal government against the relief camp workers. Thus they would be requesting reinforcements for the RCMP but balked at a suggestion by Ashton that they recruit special provincial police to keep order.

> I raised the question of augmenting their forces with special police and was immediately met by the statement that at the present time the feeling in British Columbia among all classes of people including the so-called better classes was on the side of the men

in the camps and that, therefore, they felt little help would be forthcoming. Both the Premier and the Attorney-General stated that unless some form of inquiry was held to investigate camp conditions and look into grievances little response of assistance could be expected. [8]

During the last days of March while the RCWU was busy organizing for the walkout federal officials were preparing to use troops and prison camps if necessary. Such plans were discussed at a high-level meeting of Defence Minister Grote Stirling, General McNaughton, Labour Minister W. A. Gordon and Acting Prime Minister Sir George Perley in Stirling's office on March 27. They discussed using the militia from British Columbia and elsewhere if necessary and McNaughton assured the ministers that he regarded the militia as totally dependable. McNaughton was of the opinion that the public might tolerate the establishment of prison camps.

> I said that I contemplated that if the public realized that a situation had developed which necessitated the employment of troops for the maintenance of law and order, public opinion might not react unfavourably if the further measures concerning Camps of Discipline were brought into force as a means towards keeping law and order through the segregation of those individuals whose actions were known to be subversive. [9]

Labour Minister Gordon even suggested that the DND devise a means of invoking the aid of the militia without waiting for a request from the province. [10] No decision was made on this suggestion.

Tension between the federal and provincial governments, meanwhile, was reaching a new peak. Acting Prime Minister Sir George Perley (Bennett was temporarily out of the country) was becoming very testy in denying the almost daily demands from Premier Pattullo for an independent inquiry. Perley was sharply critical of Pattullo for his refusal to put himself in the position of defending the relief camp system.

> We have repeatedly asked you to visit them and let us know in what way they could be improved. This is still the situation and we again urge you to do that. You are the head of the responsible government of your Province and surely you are not ready to admit that an investigation and report by your Government would not satisfy public opinion. [11]

This response provoked Pattullo into declaring a state of virtual cold war between the two governments.

Your Government's lack of appreciation this situation incomprehensible. If your government is under the impression that every ukase issued by your government is accepted by Public generally, *Your Government* is labouring under grave delusion. Your government is facing adverse public opinion under a system which is generally and I think properly condemned. [12]

Pattullo then went on to indicate an understanding of the existing state of mind of the camp workers and the public which the federal government appeared unable to grasp. "Some of my Ministers have visited camps and report conditions of camps as such good but that is not the point." [13] The premier also warned that the federal government would have to accept the consequences of their refusal to compromise.

It seems almost useless to continue this correspondence in light of your view but officers in your service know seriousness of conditions that if there is bloodshed and destruction of property responsibility will rest upon your government. [14]

The federal authorities may or may not have been influenced by Pattullo's outburst, but the next day they changed their minds about a commission of inquiry and began making preparations for one. [15] On April 1, an Order-in-Council, P.C. 861, was passed appointing a Royal Commission to examine conditions and complaints in DND relief camps. [16] The commission was chaired by Honourable W.A. MacDonald, lately of the Supreme Court of British Columbia. It also consisted of Charles T. McHattie, Vice-President of Galt's Limited and Chairman of the Board of the Vancouver Welfare Federation, and Rev. E.D. Braden, Organizing Chairman of the Joint Committee of Relief Camp Religious Work.

The MacDonald Commission was too little and too late to affect the situation. It was appointed on April 1 and the walkout was scheduled for April 4. General Ashton had previously reported from B.C. that an inquiry at that late date would not prevent the mass walkout "but on the other hand there was some opinion that it might create a favourable impression on the public mind." [17] It definitely did not create a favourable impression in the minds of the RCWU and their supporters. They regarded the commission as a last-minute political manoeuvre and announced that the strike would go ahead as scheduled.

It quickly became clear to the RCWU and their supporters that the terms of reference of the MacDonald Commission were too narrow to consider any of the RCWU demands. This became evident at the first public hearings of the commission in Vancouver on April 4. The commission read a letter from Ernest Cumber representing the RCWU in which he stated that the commission was only a "stop-gap" and that the issues were fifty cents per hour, release of the camps from military control, and abolition of the blacklist. The commission took the stand that, as they were empowered only to report on conditions in the camps and investigate specific complaints, the matters raised by Mr. Cumber were outside their jurisdiction. [18]

The walkout scheduled for April 4 began a few days early in some localities and was soon general throughout B.C. relief camps, though the strike had not yet materialized in Alberta. General Ashton reported to General McNaughton on April 4 that at least 1200 men had left the camps and were en route to Vancouver. Ashton estimated that the walkout would eventually number 2000 and Vancouver civic officials feared it might reach 3000 men. [19]

The B.C. and Vancouver governments announced publicly before the walkout that no relief would be provided for strikers who congregated in Vancouver. All three levels of government took measures during the first week of the strike to ensure that they had sufficient armed forces in the Vancouver vicinity and throughout the province to deal with any situation which might arise. The B.C. government sent additional provincial police to several of the camps and to some of the towns through which the strikers would travel en route to Vancouver. Vancouver municipal authorities conferred about whether it would be necessity to request the province to call upon the federal government for "aid to the civil power." They concluded that, for the time being, they could handle the situation with forces available in the Vancouver vicinity. There were at the time ninety-five city policemen, 100 provincial police, 135 RCMP and 100 special reserve constables in training, as well as about fifty more policemen who could be brought from Victoria and other nearby centres in the event of an emergency. [20]

The DND made additional preparations for the use of Permanent Force troops and the Non-Permanent Active Militia (NPAM). However, the Permanent Force was small and no more than a few hundred could be spared to deal with an emergency in Vancouver. It was not considered advisable to move NPAM from other provinces unless absolutely necessary. It would be costly and time consuming and might leave other areas of the country undermanned in the event of trouble. The strategy of General Ashton in Vancouver was to lend military facilities and technical assistance to the local authorities in the hope that it would not be necessary to call in the official armed forces. [21]

Within a week of the walkout the Vancouver authorities became very alarmed at the potentialities of the situation: evidence was growing that the strikers were better organized and more determined than they had been in the mass walkout of the previous December; and the relief camp strikers were obviously receiving more support from local trade unions and the general public than ever before.

The support extended to the strikers was indicated immediately by cash donations from several trade unions. In the first week the waterfront workers donated $800 and the Street Railway Union $117 to support the relief camp workers. [22] Donations of this nature were to continue in the weeks ahead, supplemented by generous financial assistance from the general public. A very successful "tag day," for example, was held in Vancouver and Victoria on April 13, and though it was technically illegal, the police did not interfere and more than $5,700 was collected. [23]

Support rallies, although small at first, began increasing in size very quickly. A parade in support of the strikers on April 9 was estimated by the newspapers to number 5000 people though the police claimed there were only 2000. [24]

A public meeting was held on April 19 under the sponsorship of the two Vancouver Labour Councils representing the Trades and Labour Congress (TLC) and the All-Canadian Congress of Labour (ACCL). [25] This rally of 4000-5000 people was held to support the relief camp strikers and also the striking coal miners of Corbin, a town in the Crow's Nest Pass where a bitter strike had led to massive intervention by the RCMP. The meeting included speakers from the TLC, the ACCL, the WUL, the CCF, the CCF Women's Section, the Communist Party, the RCWU, and a number of other organizations. There were reported to be forty-two organizations represented, including many unions—Waterfront and Transport Workers, Steamfitters, Building Trades, Electricians, Firemen, Miners, Lumber Workers, Sheetmetal Workers, and many others. The meeting passed resolutions calling for an end to police intervention in Corbin and abolition of the relief camps.

As the RCWU continued building public support for their cause the situation became more precarious for the authorities. Discontent went far beyond the ranks of the unemployed and what alarmed the authorities most of all was that it affected even some of the people upon whom they would have to rely in the event of major confrontations. The Vancouver city police had suffered recent pay cuts and an unpopular reorganization which made them none too

110

happy with the civic government. Some elements of the militia were now considered unreliable despite McNaughton's assurances to the contrary only a few weeks previous. The Point Grey relief camp had been the only relief camp used to train those unemployed men who had volunteered for the militia and were considered totally loyal to the authorities. Now it turned out that some were not as loyal as had been assumed.

Chief Foster of the Vancouver city police expressed fears for the loyalty of his own men. General MacBrien, Commissioner of the RCMP, visited Vancouver to assess the situation and after consultations with local police and military officials reported his fears to General Ashton who reported them in turn to McNaughton.

> MacBrien reports feeling of fear in Vancouver generally, advises getting strikers out of Vancouver at any cost. Return all men to camps without medical examination, including agitators. Foster not too sure of his own Police as following recent reorganization police are none too happy. Doubts reliability of Militia—those in relief camp at Point Grey having been influenced by general feeling. [26]

As they had in the walkout of December 1934, the strikers demanded food and shelter from the municipal and provincial authorities pending negotiations on their grievances with the federal government. These demands were refused. City Hall was less sympathetic than it had been the previous December—Mayor Louis D. Taylor had been replaced by G.G. (Gerry) McGeer, a populist similar to Pattullo in many respects but more authoritarian, irrational when annoyed or faced with opposition, and unpredictable. One day McGeer would lash out at the single unemployed and the next at the federal government. Sometimes he denounced them both simultaneously.

McGeer appears to have underestimated the strength of the strike at first and to have felt that the best strategy was to "nip the movement in the bud" even if this meant risking violent confrontation. The local DND report to NDHQ on April 9 noted that the mayor was growing impatient. "Mayor McGeer reports he is in position to cope with situation and wants showdown soon as possible." [27]

Mayor McGeer never specified what he meant by a "showdown" and the city police took no immediate action to force strikers out of Vancouver. Within a few days McGeer ceased to encourage a "showdown" and insisted that the DND take all the men back into the camps unconditionally—an irrelevant demand since they were not attempting to go back to the camps. [28] The mayor seems to have concluded that a "showdown" was inadvisable in view of the large numbers of strikers, doubts about police reliability, public sympathy for the strikers, and reports that several local trade unions were discussing sympathy strikes leading up to a general strike on May 1. [29] General Ashton reported that there were about 1700 camp strikers in Vancouver on April 19, including fifty-one who had been members of militia units at the Point Grey camp.

The relief camp strikers were mainly engaged in mass meetings, demonstrations and parades accompanied by leafletting. These events were designed to both keep up morale and inform the public of grievances and demands. They also engaged in actions designed to disrupt normal business activity. Tactics included "snake dances" through the streets, which halted traffic for brief periods, and parades through department stores which, while orderly and legal, interfered with sales and caused apprehension among businessmen. RCWU strategy was to exert enough pressure on local authorities that they, in turn, would urge the federal government to make concessions. The strategy involved avoiding violence if at all possible and, while being sufficiently disruptive to maintain the pressure, not inconveniencing the public to the point where they would be turned against the strikers' cause.

While the struggle continued in Vancouver a network of sympathizers throughout the country carried on a campaign to keep the public informed and force concessions from the federal government. The job of appealing for public support was easier than it had been in previous years. By now the federal government was under general attack by much of the press nationally for their handling of the relief camp system. There had been charges of profiteering on the part of companies selling supplies to the camps. [30] There were also press criticisms over the continuing refusal to amend the Dominion Elections Act and guarantee voting rights to relief camp workers. [31] Some daily press editorialists were even suggesting that grievances did not cease to be legitimate merely because the people concerned relied on radical or communist leadership. This point was made by the Saskatoon *Star-Phoenix* when it commented on the relief camp strike.

> Insofar as this particular trouble may be due to Communist influence, it is a case of Communist leadership being more effective than anything else that was offered. It is rather fantastic to suggest that 2,000 young and able bodied men, or any portion of that number, were intimidated into leaving the camps and going to

Vancouver. Even Communists are not such terrifying creatures as to achieve that result.[32]

The arguments between the federal and provincial authorities remained almost identical to what they had been during the December crisis and in the weeks leading up to the April 4 walkout. Provincial officials continued to argue publicly and privately for a federal work and wages programme while refusing to give relief to the men and insisting they go back to the camps. The Bennett government refused any concessions whatsoever aside from the last-minute appointment of a commission of inquiry with no mandate to consider the main grievances of the camp workers. Federal officials also continued to insist that law and order were a provincial responsibility but that they were prepared to employ troops and establish prison camps if requested to do so by the province.

The federal strategy seems to have been to wait out the crisis in the hope that the strikers' declining financial resources coupled with a loss of morale would eventually compel them to return to the camps under terms acceptable to the DND. If the strikers became frustrated to the point where there were outbreaks of violence it appeared that the local and provincial authorities would have to make common cause with the federal government in rallying public opinion to the forces of law and order. Either the gradual collapse of the strike or the necessity to forcefully suppress acts of violence could be considered a victory for the federal government.

By the beginning of the third week of the strike the situation had reached a stalemate in Vancouver. Officials from all three levels of government agreed privately that the public was critical of the relief camp system and supported at least some of the demands of the RCWU. The same was true of the press, the trade unions, the teachers' associations, and a diversity of other mass organizations. Yet the Bennett regime refused a single concession and the civic and provincial authorities held firm in refusing relief to the camp workers in Vancouver.

The RCWU and the strikers were faced with a dilemma. They were getting nowhere with their demands and their financial resources would soon run out. They were not in a normal trade union situation whereby they could close down a factory or an office and then passively wait until economic necessity compelled the employer to bargain seriously. The governments concerned were not suffering economic losses, at least in the immediate sense, by the fact that the men were not working in the camps. This meant the strikers had to risk escalating their disruptive tactics to the point where influential sections of the community would demand an acceptable settlement to get the strikers out of Vancouver. While doing so, they also had to maintain the sympathy of a majority of the public and especially a majority within the trade unions and allied organizations. This ruled out a resort to violence and meant that disruptive tactics had to be planned with great care and carried out peacefully and with great discipline. In the short term a sympathetic public was more important to the strikers than to the federal government.

The next move in the political chess game was up to the RCWU and their supporters. They rose to the occasion and in the last days of April carried out a brilliant escalation of their disruptive tactics and simultaneously made a successful bid for an even greater demonstration of public support.

Footnotes

1. Public Archives of Canada (PAC), *McNaughton Papers,* File 359, Vol. 2, Ashton to Secretary of DND, January 5, 1935.
2. *Ibid.,* File 359 (Vol. 2), DOC 11 to Adjutant-General, February 16, 1935.
3. *Ibid.,* File 359 (Vol. 2), McNaughton to Dickson, February 6, 1935.
4. *Ibid.,* File 359 (Vol. 2), Farris to Bennett, February 25, 1935.
5. Archives of Saskatchewan (A.S.), Regina Riot Inquiry Commission (RRIC) Record of Proceedings, Vol. 7, p. 64. This conference is also discussed in Gladys Stone, *The Regina Riot: 1935,* unpublished M.A. thesis, University of Saskatchewan, 1967, pp. 13-15.
6. *Ibid.*
7. *McNaughton Papers, op.cit.,* File 359 (Vol. 2), Ashton to McNaughton, March 16, 1935.
8. *Ibid.,* File 359 (Vol. 2), Ashton to McNaughton, March 25, 1935.
9. *Ibid.,* File 359 (Vol. 2), McNaughton Memorandum, March 27, 1935.
10. *Ibid.* The accepted practice was that federal authorities would not use the militia "in aid to the civil power" unless requested to do so by the Attorney-General of a province.
11. *Ibid.,* File 359 (Vol. 2), Perley to Pattullo, March 27, 1935.
12. *Ibid.,* File 359 (Vol. 2), Pattullo to Perley, March 27, 1935.
13. *Ibid.*
14. *Ibid.*
15. *Ibid.,* File 359 (Vol. 2), McNaughton Memorandum, March 28, 1935.
16. House of Commons *Debates,* Vol. III, pp. 2278-79, April 1, 1935.
17. *McNaughton Papers, op.cit.,* File 359 (Vol. 2), McNaughton Memorandum, March 28, 1935.

18. *Ibid.*, File 359 (Vol. 2), McNaughton Memorandum, April 4, 1935.
19. *Ibid.*
20. *Ibid.*, Vol. 61, File 380 (B), DOC 11 to C.G.S., April 4, 1935.
21. *Ibid.*, File 359 (Vol. 2), Ashton to McNaughton, April 5, 1935.
22. *Ibid.*, Vol. 51, File 380 (B), M.D. 11 to A.G., April 11, 1935.
23. *Ibid.*, Vol. 61, File 380 (B), M.D. 11 to CGS, April 30, 1935.
24. *Ibid.*, Vol. 61, File 3580 (B) M.D. 11 to A.G., April 20, 1935.
25. *Ibid.*, Vol. 61, File 380 (B), M.D. 11 to CGS, April 20, 22, 23, 1935.
26. *Ibid.*, Vol. 61, File 380 (B), McNaughton Memorandum, April 18, 1935.
27. *Ibid.*, Vol. 61, File 380 (B), DOC 11 to A.G., April 9, 1935.
28. *Ibid.*, Vol. 61, File 380 (B), DOC 11 to A.G. April 12, 1935.
29. *Ibid.*
30. Regina *Leader-Post*, March 17, 1935.
31. *Ibid.*
32. Saskatoon *Star-Phoenix*, April 29, 1935.

"Tin canning" for donations for the Relief Camp Workers' Union, Victoria, 1935. (Photo #A-1657, Provincial Archives of B.C.)

Helena Guthridge addressing a rally for the relief camp strikers at the Powell Street Grounds in Vancouver, April 1935. Guthridge was an activist in the CCF and the women's movement. For a time she was a Vancouver Alderwoman. (Photo #C-7954, Provincial Archives of B.C.)

116

May Day 1935. A depiction of Mayor McGeer reading the Riot Act in front of the Vancouver Cenotaph a week earlier. (Photo #8809, Vancouver Public Library)

The youth contingent, Vancouver, May Day 1935. (Photo #8796, Vancouver Public Library)

117

May Day 1935. An estimated 1000-3000 students walked out of Vancouver schools in support of the relief camp strikers, many of them accompanied by their teachers. (Photo #8788, Vancouver Public Library)

An estimated 35,000 people attended the rally in Stanley Park in support of the relief camp strikers following the Vancouver May Day parade, 1935. (Photo #8826, Vancouver Public Library)

118

Mothers parade in support of the relief camp strikers, Vancouver, 1935. (Photo #8798, Vancouver Public Library)

Part of the Italian contingent in the 1935 May Day parade, Vancouver. (Photo #8792, Vancouver Public Library)

The trekkers arrive in Regina. (Photo #C-24840, Public Archives of Canada)

The Regina Riot, July 1, 1935. (Photo #R-B171(3), Saskatchewan Archives)

Veterans of the 1930s struggles meet the 1980s unemployed on Parliament Hill, Ottawa, June 1985. (Photo: Dale Lakevold, *Briarpatch* magazine)

Bill Gilbey at the commemorative trek in Ottawa, 1985. Gilbey was a founder and organizer of the RCWU in the early 1930s. He later served overseas in World War II and has spent all of the years since in the trade union movement. He is a past president of the Saskatchewan Federation of Labour. (Photo: *Briarpatch* magazine)

Robert (Doc) Savage, one of the leaders of the On-to-Ottawa Trek and the only surviving member of the eight-man Trek delegation who met with Prime Minister Bennett and his Cabinet in Ottawa on June 22, 1935. This photo was taken in June 1985 when Savage again travelled to Ottawa as part of the commemorative trek. (Photo: E. Smillie, *Briarpatch* magazine)

Robert (Bobby) Jackson, one of the leaders of the On-to-Ottawa Trek of 1935 and the commemorative trek in 1985. "The sad goddamned situation is that our sons and daughters are now looking for jobs the way we did fifty years ago." (Photo: E. Smillie, *Briarpatch* magazine)

123

Arthur H. (Slim) Evans, 1890-1944, the Relief Camp
Workers' Union's chief organizer and main leader of the
On-to-Ottawa Trek of 1935. (Photo courtesy of Jean
Evans Sheils)

CHAPTER VII

The Struggle Escalates and the Trek Begins

The Relief Camp Workers' Union and their supporters suddenly escalated their tactics on April 23, 1935, when several hundred strikers occupied the ground floor of the Hudson's Bay Company department store in downtown Vancouver. When city police were sent in to evict the strikers a battle erupted which resulted in injuries to a number of strikers and police, several arrests, and considerable damage.

Following the struggle at the Hudson's Bay store a large crowd of strikers and sympathizers gathered at Victory Square in the downtown area. They held a public meeting and chose a delegation of strikers to seek an interview with Mayor McGeer. A second delegation of non-striking citizens was then despatched to City Hall accompanied by Harold Winch, MLA. In response, McGeer agreed to go down to the meeting at Victory Square. Shortly after arriving, however, he read the Riot Act from the Cenotaph. By now the crowd was surrounded by large contingents of RCMP, provincial, and city police, many of them mounted. The crowd was allowed to march peacefully out of the square after brief negotiations between Harold Winch and Police Chief Foster. Public meetings were then held in the various halls serving as strike headquarters and Mayor McGeer was roundly denounced. He had clearly shown his hand and would henceforth be regarded as an inveterate enemy of the relief camp strikers.

That same evening city and provincial police raided two of the RCWU headquarters and seized banners, placards, and files. A meeting to protest these raids was held shortly afterwards on Hastings

Street and was broken up by police with more injuries and arrests. [1]
The next day McGeer declared that all public meetings, parades
and demonstrations would be banned in the future—a threat which
the city made no attempt to enforce in the days ahead. [2] To attempt
to enforce such a ban at this stage would probably have led to
massive civil disobedience, bloodshed on a considerable scale, and
a city beyond the control of the authorities. McGeer also launched
a public attack on the RCWU and declared the relief camp strike
to be part of a communist conspiracy with revolutionary aims. [3] The
charges of a communist conspiracy would be repeated many times
by McGeer over the next few weeks.

The violent confrontation at the Hudson's Bay store and the
repeated charges of a communist conspiracy did not bring about
the backlash against the strikers which McGeer may have envisioned.
Even much of the daily press continued to support the relief camp
workers. On April 24 Bob Bouchette, a columnist for the Vancouver
Sun, blamed all three levels of government for the disturbances at
the store and the clashes with the police later in the day. It is worth
quoting Bouchette's arguments at some length because they are
representative of the feelings of many journalists and others, who,
while not generally left-wing in their political views, regarded the
relief camp workers as having very good reasons for militant action.

> Before you condemn these men for whatever violence was done
> by them it might be a good idea to review the record of their
> activities since they walked out of the relief camps and came to
> Vancouver.
>
> It is well to sift the evidence to determine whether the relief
> camp strikers are dangerous, irreconcilable or victims of a situation.
>
> There was no complaint with respect to the conduct of the
> men during the first couple of weeks of their stay here. They
> presented their demands with dignity and restraint and when
> they were refused flatly, disowned by city, province, and Dominion,
> they continued to advertise their case peaceably.
>
> But they were getting hungrier. They asked the city for a
> permit to hold a tag day. Turned down, they held the tag day
> anyway and the people of Vancouver showed how they felt towards
> them by contributing the largest sum ever raised in this manner
> in British Columbia.
>
> Then the strikers were informed that they must hold no parades.
> Apparently it was the purpose of the authorities to take away
> from disenfranchised, jobless young men the only means through
> which they may appeal to the public. Not only were they denied

food and shelter, but their right of demonstration, traditionally accorded to a free citizenry, was refused them.

Under ordinary circumstances that would be sufficient to annoy any group of human beings. To a half-starved body of men looking into a future barren of hope it must have been galling.[4]

Bouchette's sentiments about the escalation of events in Vancouver were echoed by many columnists and editorialists throughout the country. In an editorial entitled "Vancouver Reads Riot Act" the Ottawa *Citizen* took the authorities to task for offering people no hope and then blaming the victims when they rebelled.

It is not human to put up with such conditions as the inmates of relief camps are supposed to put up with month after month and year after year. For making a fuss they are called "Reds." But if they did not make a fuss they would be less than human.[5]

There was one attempt to work out a compromise settlement on April 25 when the Vancouver Trades and Labour Council and Mayor McGeer cooperated in calling a meeting for this purpose. The meeting was attended by McGeer, General Ashton, Chief of Police Foster, three representatives of the Vancouver TLC, CCF MLA's Harold Winch and Bert Price, CCF M.P., Angus MacInnis, and four representatives of the RCWU. No agreement could be reached.

The same afternoon a mass meeting of strikers and sympathizers was held on the Cambie Street grounds. The crowd, estimated at 7000, passed a resolution to be sent to the prime minister which was critical of all levels of government and supportive of the demands of the strikers.

We, 7000 Vancouver citizens, condemn the policy of Municipal, Provincial and Federal Governments in handling of Relief Camp problems and demand immediate relief for the strikers and immediate opening of negotiations on their seven demands.[6]

The RCWU followed up on the mass meeting with plans for bigger and more effective demonstrations of public support. On the night of April 25 the Longshoremen's Union voted to stage a sympathy strike for one hour on April 29 and to encourage other unions to do likewise. They also donated one per cent of a month's pay, between $400 and $500 in total, to the RCWU strike fund. There were also discussions among Longshoremen and in other unions as well of the possibility of a one-day general strike in support of RCWU demands to be held either on May 1 or at a later date.

In advocating more militant actions the RCWU and their supporters ran into considerable trouble with the more conservative among the leaders of the local Trades and Labour Council (TLC) and the CCF. There was considerable sympathy for the RCWU cause among the members of both these organizations, but the leaders were split. The more left-wing TLC and CCF leaders had no problem lending their full support; the more conservative leaders sympathized with the struggle, as did most of the public, but they had an aversion to general strikes, militant demonstrations, or any activities which had a remote resemblance to civil disobedience.

These disagreements over tactics and strategy led to considerable tension within trade union and political circles in Vancouver. The TLC leadership opposed even a one hour work stoppage and were adamantly opposed to the idea of a general strike. The more conservative CCF leaders took a similar attitude. They were obsessed with the search for compromise to the point where they emphasized a quick and peaceful solution even if it meant sacrificing most of the demands of the relief camp workers. It was the TLC leadership which called the April 25 meeting with Mayor McGeer and advocated concessions which brought criticism from RCWU supporters at some of their strategy meetings. TLC leaders were accused of attempting to split the ranks of the relief camp strikers and prevent sympathetic strike action by Vancouver trade unionists.[7]

Many of the CCF leaders were reluctant to cooperate too closely with the RCWU for fear of being identified with the communists. This reflected a sectarian attitude towards the Communist Party and in some cases an anti-communist bias common among many CCF activists. Many communists harboured similar sectarian attitudes towards the CCF. The existence of ideological and political tensions and rivalry required great patience and skill on the part of RCWU leaders to maintain the solidarity of their support coalition while at the same time carrying through with the militant tactics which the situation required.

That the opinion of the broadly progressive community remained behind the strikers is indicated by a mass meeting under the auspices of the Women's CCF held at Moose Hall on the night of the Longshoremen's meeting. Speakers included the secretaries of the RCWU, the Women's Labour League, the Vancouver Parent-Teachers' Association, the British Columbia Parent-Teachers' Association, the CCF, and the New Era League, all of whom advocated continuation of the strike and abolition of the relief camps. The meeting decided that the CCF women sponsor a parade and mass rally at the Vancouver

Arena on Sunday, April 28, preceded by a petition and tag day. The tags would ask, "Are our sons criminals?"[8]

The parade and rally turned out to be a tremendous demonstration of public support for the relief camp strikers. A crowd, estimated by DND officials at 15,000 and by RCWU leaders at close to 20,000, marched from the Cambie Street grounds to the Vancouver Arena. Speakers included Dr. Lyle Telford, CCF provincial leader; Harold Winch, MLA and a future Leader of the British Columbia CCF, Tom Uphill, MLA (Independent labour); Arnold Webster, prominent CCF high school teacher; Pete Munroe of the Street Railway Union; and Mr. Ross of the Waterfront Workers. Munroe announced that his organization had donated $1180 to the strike fund and the meeting itself collected another $1527.44.[9] All speakers again called for a continuation of the strike and abolition of the relief camps.

DND officials were concerned at the massive show of public support and alarmed at the tone of the speakers. Pete Munroe suggested that "if necessary we will have to fight it out in the streets."[10] Harold Winch declared that some people might die before the strike was over and implied that it might be necessary to meet force with force. "If authorities use the mailed fist it is time the people took off their gloves also."[11] Ross of the Waterfront Workers announced that the trade unions were being canvassed on the possibility of a general strike to force the closing of the camps. The meeting passed a resolution supporting the strikers and promising similar demonstrations of support until the strike was settled on acceptable terms.

The one-hour sympathy strike of April 29 was a much more qualified success than the mass meetings which preceded it. The top officers of the Trades and Labour Council had so effectively opposed the work stoppage that only a few of the more left-wing unions participated. Nonetheless, about 1000 trade unionists did stop work for one hour despite TLC opposition. They were mainly Longshoremen but also included members of the Seafarers' Industrial Union, the Export Logging Union and scattered members of other unions. The RCWU organized a parade of 3000 sympathizers who marched to the waterfront to thank the Longshoremen for their support.[12]

After April 29 the RCWU, nearly all left-wing organizations, and many trade unions throughout Vancouver put on a tremendous drive for a show of strength on May Day. They hoped for one of the largest demonstrations in the history of Vancouver. The organized unemployed knew they had massive public support and they wanted to demonstrate it beyond a shadow of doubt to all politicians and especially to the Bennett government.

If Bennett and his ministers had been paying attention to their correspondence they would have known the extent to which the public had lost confidence in the relief camp system and the general economic strategy of their government. A wide variety of individuals and organizations, many of them not known for their left-wing sympathies or progressive leanings, had been inundating the prime minister's office with condemnation of the relief camp system. This response came from across the country but especially from Vancouver, and the letters had been increasing in number and getting more insistent in tone throughout the spring of 1935.

One such message was sent to Bennett by the Vancouver branch of the Women's Christian Temperance Union.

> Realizing that Relief Camps are not in the best interests of our Canadian men, we, the Vancouver District Women's Christian Temperance Union urge the abolition of the Unemployment Camps and the Substitution of work with adequate remuneration. [13]

Similar sentiments were expressed in a telegram from T. Jean Ralston on behalf of "the local Council of Women of Vancouver and twelve other organizations" received by Acting Prime Minister Perley on April 25:

> The protest of Camp men is a logical outcome of policy extending over three years which has deprived Canadian men of hope and self-expression. The influence of present policy is such that it imperils the welfare of all Canadian citizens. [14]

Similar telegrams and letters were received in the prime minister's office on behalf of the Victoria Liberal Women's Forum on April 12, the General Ministerial Association of greater Vancouver on April 25, the Vancouver Presbytery of the United Church on April 26, the British Columbia Parent-Teachers' Association on April 27, the boards of St. Giles United Church and Chown United Church on April 28, the annual meeting of the British Columbia Teachers' Federation on April 30, and from the Loyal Orange Association, Vancouver, LOL No. 1, on April 30. [15] Scores of similar messages were received from labour councils, trade union locals and other labour bodies in the Victoria, Vancouver and lower mainland areas.

Federal ministers were also receiving messages from prominent Conservatives and people close to the party warning them that

130

public opinion was with the relief camp workers and something positive must be done. One was from H.H. Stevens, former minister of trade and commerce, who had split with the Bennett cabinet over the controversy surrounding the Price Spreads Commission. [16] Stevens had been critical of the relief camp system before and now he insisted that the camps be abolished altogether in favour of a work and wages alternative.

> It is not reasonable to expect thousands of young, healthy men, many of them well educated, to submit indefinitely to confinement to camps on a subsistence basis. It is not natural, and in my opinion the Federal Parliament and the Federal Government must recognize that simple truth. [17]

Stevens also included in his communication a paragraph from a letter he had received from "a prominent and conservative businessman of Vancouver and former President of the Board of Trade and Manufacturers' Association." The letter spoke highly of the relief camp strikers and their motivations.

> They are on the average bright, healthy, clean-looking young boys, and might be either your sons or mine, and it is just too bad the buck is passed between the three governing bodies to the extent it has been. These young men will not stay in camps and be deprived of taking their share in work and wages with others. [18]

There were numerous letters of this nature. Lieutenant Colonel H.E. Lyon (retired) of Vancouver, for instance, wrote, "I can assure you that the people are behind these boys and that the use of force will not be tolerated." [19] T.H. Wilkinson of British Columbia Lumber and Shingle Manufacturers Limited enclosed a column from the Vancouver *Sun* favourable to the strikers and warned of trouble to come. [20] Right Reverend Charles D. Schofield, D.D., Anglican Bishop of British Columbia, offered the assistance of the clergy to improve camp conditions and suggested more liberal regulations in the camps. [21]

Even extreme anti-communists who were paranoid about the possibility of revolution had the insight to see that the situation had become intolerable to the point where an alternative to the camps was essential. One such was Elmo Marshal, Chairman of the Vancouver Conservative Joint Council. Marshall wrote the prime minister an alarming letter about the revolutionary possibilities in British Columbia.

Dr. Lyle Telford-Pritchard-Winch, and other supposed C.C.F'ers. but who are in reality, as red as the reddest have literally bulldozed the C.C.F. organizations into a stand of practical advocacy of revolution. [22]

Marshal claimed that the communists were following almost word for word the tactics he had read about "in that famous RED BOOK of tactics and advice issued by the THIRD INTERNATIONAL" [23] (emphasis in original). While alleging that the communists and perhaps even the CCF were attempting to foment revolution, Marshal stated that public sympathy was with the strikers and advocated an immediate federal-provincial programme of public works to provide work and wages for the unemployed in the Vancouver area. Marshal concluded his letter with emphasis on the gravity of the situation as he saw it.

am deeply in earnest about this condition. It is very serious— more so than those down east realize. Communistic elements have taken control, backed by the C.C.F., and even our Ministerial friends in some cases have not been above indulging in rabid tirades. [24]

By the end of April there was no excuse for any politician at any level of government to be unaware not only of the grievances of the relief camp workers but also of the fact that the public overwhelmingly supported their cause. Mayor McGeer and the federal authorities disagreed about the value of the camps but they cooperated in launching public attacks portraying the strike as a communist conspiracy to foment revolution. McGeer made a radio broadcast for that purpose on April 27 and Ashton reported the event to McNaughton.

General Ashton regards Mayor's broadcast as very helpful, the Mayor stating that the British Columbia Camp Workers' Union definitely communistic from its inception and had promised the men from camps their walkout would be supported by a general strike leading to a revolution. [25]

Acting Prime Minister Perley followed up McGeer's broadcast with a statement of his own in which he portrayed the strike as "part of a carefully staged demonstration by communistic and subversive organizations who seek to fundamentally alter and destroy the existing basis of authority." [26] Perley also claimed that most relief camp strikers had been forced by the communists to leave the camps against their will and appealed to the citizenry to stand behind the government while the economy recovered.

> The action of the subversive organizations in depriving the men of the care which has been offered, and they are being used without regard to their own interests in furthering the purpose of upsetting law and order. The Dominion Government is well aware that the great majority of the men who are now congregated in Vancouver are there under the militant coercion of agitators. All citizens should recognize the facts of the situation and should steadfastly support the efforts which are being made to stimulate the orderly recovery of industry in Canada which is now in process.[27]

Provincial, civic and federal leaders were united in attempting to turn the public against the RCWU by portraying them as part of a revolutionary communist conspiracy. But they could not maintain a united front before the public. Civic and provincial officials would not be caught in the political trap of identifying with a discredited federal regime and they continued to insist that the relief camps be replaced by a federal work and wages programme. Neither Pattullo nor McGeer would publicly request the federal government to use armed force against the strikers though they did not oppose force in principle. And both were becoming increasingly annoyed at repeated federal offers to assist provincial authorities with force to maintain law and order while continuing to reject out of hand a work and wages programme. McGeer blasted the federal government publicly after Acting Prime Minister Perley had renewed such an offer on April 27.

> In plain language that means that if the government of British Columbia will inform the national government it cannot maintain order, the national government will take charge of the province under the authority of martial law. Our national government is apparently anxious to declare its willingness to wage war on people but unfortunately unwilling to declare its willingness to wage war on poverty.[28]

The time had passed when federal authorities could have used force with impunity. The Bennett government was becoming so politically isolated that even the old battle cry of "law and order" had lost its appeal.

The big test of public support for the single unemployed came on May 1 when May Day parades, rallies and demonstrations were held in most of the major cities of Canada. By far the largest parade and rally took place in Vancouver, where May Day observers focused around the issue of the relief camp strikers. The strikers and thousands upon thousands of their sympathizers gathered at the Cambie Street grounds and marched to Stanley Park where they were joined by thousands more for speeches. Estimates of the numbers participating varied. *The Relief Camp Worker* estimated 15,000 in the parade and 35,000 at Stanley Park. [29] General Ashton reported to McNaughton that there were 12,000 in the parade and 14,000 at the park. Police Chief Foster, who had thirty-five of his undercover agents in Stanley Park, reported to Mayor McGeer that there were at least 14,000 in the procession and 20,000 at the park, "but it is claimed by those participating, and even by a great many of our own men, that that number was greatly exceeded." [30] A report from one police agent estimated 23,000 in the parade and 28,000 at the park. [31]

What was encouraging about the May Day turnout, aside from the numbers, was the cross-section of the population which turned out. Trade unionists were well represented and, despite TLC opposition, a number of unions also participated in a one-day work stoppage. These included the Longshoremen, the Boilermakers Union, the Seafarers Industrial Union, the Coastwise Freight Handlers Union, and the Log Boom Union. The ports of Vancouver and New Westminster were idle. Other unions with official contingents in the parade, though they did not join the work stoppage, included the Carpenters and Joiners, the Fishermen and Cannery Workers' Industrial Union, the Food Workers, the Mine Workers Union of Canada, and the Lumber Workers.

In addition to the RCWU and the various unemployed associations in the Vancouver area, there were contingents from half a dozen ethnic groups, the Farmers' Unity League, the Workers' Ex-Servicemen's League, the League Against War and Fascism, and many others. High school students (the RCWU claimed 3000 while the federal officials estimated 1000) walked out of the schools to join the demonstration. [32] They had been organized by the Student League of Canada, the Young Socialist League, and the Co-operative Commonwealth Youth. They were joined by sympathetic high school teachers. The majority at the parade and rally were not part of any official contingent but sympathetic members of the public.

The May Day events were hailed as an overwhelming demonstration of public support for the cause of the single unemployed; even their enemies had to admit it. On the surface the situation in early May looked good for the strikers. Hardly any had returned to the camps and very few had left Vancouver individually in search of jobs elsewhere even though many often left the camps for that purpose in the spring of the year. And public support seemed to be holding firm or even increasing.

The problem was that demonstrations of public support alone were not enough. All three levels of government refused to budge. Even with public support the strikers were running extremely short of funds and it was becoming more difficult to maintain morale. Most of the men had been demonstrating, marching, and attending meetings for nearly a month and still there were no concessions in sight. The one action which might have compelled the authorities to negotiate, a general strike involving most of the major unions in the Vancouver area, had not materialized and it did not appear likely that it would. Even some of the leaders were becoming discouraged. There were also political tensions among the strikers and their supporters and sympathizers. There was friction between the CCF and the communists and a constant struggle between the radical and conservative elements of the labour movement. Both the local TLC leadership and elements within the CCF leadership were wavering and uncertain in their support. [33]

The leadership of the RCWU was extremely resourceful in devising tactics to maintain public support and keep up morale. They continued to agitate for a general strike and to hold out hope for such an action. They held "speakers' schools" to give the secondary leadership and rank and file an elementary knowledge of public speaking. Strikers then spoke to scores of union meetings and small neighbourhood meetings in every district of Vancouver and the surrounding area to explain their point of view to the public.

The RCWU also sponsored a "straw vote" preceded by an intensive canvass of the Vancouver area asking people whether they supported the abolition of the relief camps and the granting of immediate relief to the strikers. People then voted on the question in an informal plebiscite on May 10. There were 27,647 votes cast and nearly all favoured abolishing the camps and granting immediate relief to the strikers. The vote was regarded as an accurate reflection of public opinion and Mayor McGeer even brought the matter to the attention of Prime Minister Bennett. "The report of the vote indicates that public opinion in Vancouver is overwhelmingly against relief camp system and equally in favour of work and wages program." [34]

Another event which helped lend credibility to the strikers' cause was the formation of what became known as the Mothers' Committee, which was originally initiated by women in the CCF and eventually involved several womens' organizations and concerned individuals. The Mothers' Committee provided housing for some strikers, collected money, held rallies and picnics, and campaigned for abolition of the relief camps. On May 11 the Committee held a tag day which raised $957 for the strikers. On May 12, Mothers' Day, they held a parade and rally at Stanley Park, attracting a crowd estimated at 4000-7000.[36]

While activities of this nature continued in Vancouver the civic authorities began a national advertising campaign designed to put public pressure on the federal government for a work and wages programme. They ran an editorial from the Vancouver *Daily Province* as an advertisement in the daily newspapers of most major cities. The editorial was mildly critical of the strikers and advised them to return to the camps on the grounds that nothing more could be accomplished in Vancouver. But the harshest criticism was directed at the federal government. It was claimed that Bennett's so-called "New Deal," which the government had been busy getting through Parliament, looked good for the future but that there were no plans for dealing with the immediate and critical problems facing the country.

> But while it [the government] dreams of the future, it forgets that there is a fire burning now that must be extinguished or there will be no future of the sort it dreams about.
> There is an unemployment emergency—now.
> There is an unemployment crisis—now.
> And it demands a remedy—now.
> And the remedy cannot come through a futile squabble between Ottawa and Victoria over jurisdiction. It can come only through an honest and effective attempt to apply the waiting labour to the millions of dollars of work that is crying out to be done.[37]

The *Daily Province* editorial was not only carried as an advertisement in most daily newspapers, but many also editorially demanded action from the federal government. Much was made of the fact that the *Daily Province* was generally considered a Conservative newspaper.

The unpopularity of the Bennett Government across Canada and the public support for their cause, especially in Vancouver, were good for the morale of the camp strikers. But they were no substitute for material support, and financial resources were almost depleted by the middle of May. A Vancouver city police undercover agent estimated on May 12 that the strikers' funds would be exhausted by May 16 and that the strike might collapse because of lack of resources and declining morale by May 20.[38]

The assessment by the police agent was probably accurate. Beginning on May 16 the strikers took a series of actions designed to replenish their resources and force an end to the stalemate. The first was a mass meeting at the Cambie Street grounds to be followed by a parade to City Hall. The leaflet advertising the meeting emphasized the necessity for additional resources if the strike was to continue.

> The Camp Boys are now with their backs to the wall. Their funds are totally exhausted, they cannot ask the people of Vancouver to take them into their homes and dig out of their hard-earned wages financial support for the carrying on of this strike. They must obtain relief and work through the agencies responsible for the conditions that have been forced upon them.[39]

The leaflet went on to call upon Vancouver citizens to demonstrate mass support "to compel a showdown on the question of the Camps."[40]

The mass meeting, estimated by the RCWU at 7000-8000 and reported by General Ashton to be 3500, reiterated the usual demands but also demanded immediate relief from the city. They marched to City Hall, tying up downtown traffic for some time, while a delegation took their demands to Mayor McGeer. McGeer refused civic relief but sent a telegram to Bennett demanding immediate federal relief pending settlement of the dispute.[41] The telegram was read to the demonstrators and they eventually dispersed after severe criticism of the mayor for passing the buck once again.

The events of May 16 demonstrated once again what was becoming increasingly obvious to the strikers. Mass rallies and demonstrations alone were not going to get immediate relief for the strikers or get the federal authorities to the negotiating table. More militant tactics would be necessary.

The strikers' Strategy Committee formulated a plan to be put into action on May 18, which was a Saturday when many people would be off work and congregated in the downtown area.[42] The plan was to occupy the Vancouver City Museum, located above the main branch of the public library. The men would stay in the museum until the city agreed to grant some relief. The assumption, which turned out to be correct, was that the police would not attempt to evict the men by force out of fear that some of the irreplaceable exhibits would be damaged or destroyed during the course of the struggle.

After meeting at the Ukrainian Labour Temple, which served as one of their headquarters, the strikers divided into four divisions and proceeded to march to different destinations: one to Spenders' store, another to Woodward's store, and a third to the West Vancouver

Ferry. These three divisions were intended to deflect the attention of the police. The fourth division marched on a route which took them past the public library—which had never before been a target for demonstration. They merely turned when they reached the library and walked up the unguarded staircase to the museum. Within minutes the staff and the few visitors had been ushered out of the premises and several hundred strikers were in firm control of the museum.

The other three contingents then converged on the vicinity of the museum, bringing crowds of sympathizers with them. A telephone campaign alerted the newspapers, radio stations, trade unions, and other organizations and individuals who might either publicize the event or lend support. Soon many thousands of people were congregated in downtown Vancouver and traffic had ground to a halt. Sympathetic demonstrations took place outside the public library and in front of City Hall. Some estimate the total crowd in the downtown core at 20,000 at its peak. [43] Food, coffee, and cigarettes were collected and passed up to the strikers in baskets attached to ropes.

The strikers occupied the City Museum for approximately six hours, during which time a delegation of strikers located Mayor McGeer and Police Chief Foster and carried on negotiations for the granting of municipal relief in return for evacuation of the museum. McGeer finally promised that the city would provide funds for two days food and accommodation for all strikers. The City Museum was evacuated peacefully.

The relief camp workers hailed the occupation as a victory. It was the first concession of any significance from any level of government since the strike had begun on April 4. This victory was followed up when supporters of the Mothers' Committee occupied part of police headquarters on May 20 until they were promised one additional day of badly needed relief for the strikers. However, these victories were by no means enough by themselves to maintain the strike for long. The camp workers still hoped for sympathy strikes by the Longshoremen and other unions. Something more drastic appeared necessary.

Though a general strike appeared improbable, there were several labour disputes going on in B.C. which made a strike not outside the realm of the possible. Both the Longshoremen and Seafarer's Industrial Union were in the midst of negotiations with employers over economic issues and union recognition and the Seafarer's struck Union Steamships from May 23 to May 28. Should the Longshoremen also go out they could engage in joint demonstrations with the relief camp workers. There were also strikes and lockouts involving metal workers and pulp and paper workers at Bridgewater and Powell River, respectively. Both involved confrontations between strikers and police and the authorities feared that police reinforcements would be required. The whole situation was potentially explosive and this made the local authorities more anxious than ever to get the single unemployed out of Vancouver as quickly as possible.

Mayor McGeer made several new attempts to get the strikers out of town. He pressured DND officials to establish a special camp in the Vancouver vicinity where the men could be housed and fed pending settlement of their grievances. The proposal was rejected partly for practical reasons but also because the DND opposed any concessions on principle. They feared it would be claimed as a victory by the RCWU.[44] McGeer then proposed to the RCWU that the strikers return to the camps and leave a delegation in Vancouver to continue pressing for federal concessions. He would later make the same proposal with the added suggestion that the city would finance a delegation of three RCWU representatives to travel to Ottawa if the strikers returned to the camps. Both proposals were rejected by mass meetings of the strikers.[45]

The federal government would not make concessions and the strikers would not return to the camps without them. All three levels of government then resorted to a firmer line. On May 22 civic officials made yet another announcement that no more parades or open air meetings would be tolerated. McGeer also informed a delegation of strikers of Ottawa's offer to use force if called upon to do so by the province.[46] He also charged collusion between the "international money power" and the "Reds" to cause chaos and prevent a federal election.

> Certainly there is no reason on the part of the international bankers to complain if revolution and chaos should set off the need for a military dictatorship. That would avoid the danger of a change of government which is bound to follow a general election.
>
> The records of history are replete with instances where money power has joined with Communists to foment revolutions as a means of maintaining money power in control of humanity. Revolution and war are their trump cards and they will not hesitate to play them.
>
> Whether or not it is assisted by money power, the fact remains that Communism in its most evil form and well financed, has reared its ugly and vicious head in our community.[47]

McGeer was apparently a believer in the conspiracy theory of history which would later be popular with the more obscurantist elements of Social Credit.

Provincial officials also began to crack down on the RCWU and their supporters during the last week of May. Ernest Cumber, general secretary of the RCWU, was arrested on a charge of obtaining relief under false pretenses. [48] Cumber, who had been blacklisted, had entered a camp under a false name, a common practice among RCWU organizers. The first trial ended on May 27 when the jury could not reach agreement. Another immediately afterwards ended in the same result. In June Cumber was again arrested under Section 98 of the Criminal Code.

During the last week of May, federal and provincial officials also renewed their discussions about the possibility of establishing prison camps. [49] The B.C. government secured Pierat Island for the purposes of a provincial prison camp but did not get around to passing the required legislation. [50] General Ashton and the DND encouraged provincial activity along these lines.

> Consider in the light Public opinion being adverse to present Camp system under Defence Department prefer such disciplining measure be under Provincial control. [51]

By the last week of May demoralization had become evident among many strikers. The police were much more in evidence, meaning that the city intended to enforce its ban on outdoor rallies and demonstrations and to prevent picketing of the offices where men could apply for reinstatement in the camps. [52] As well, the strike by Longshoremen expected for May 27 would not materialize until June 6. [53] The camp workers had been counting on making common cause with the Longshoremen.

Another factor which made it more difficult to hold the strike together was increasing friction between the CCF and the communists. The more cautious among the CCF leaders were beginning to get cold feet in their support for the strike. Dr. Lyle Telford, CCF Provincial Leader, was openly critical of the RCWU leadership in a radio address on May 24.

> They (the leaders) are not camp strikers, they are mainly occupied with the task of getting these boys to do something dangerous in the name of strike action. [54]

140

Aside from the fact that it was not true, Telford's statement probably sowed considerable discord among strike sympathizers. One of the police agents who had infiltrated the ranks of the relief camp strikers regarded Telford's statement as a factor in weakening the strike. "Telford's attacks on these leaders did a lot to split things up."[55]

That a number of the strikers were weakening was indicated by the fact that some were returning to the camps and many were catching freights individually and in small groups to "ride the rods" in search of jobs as they were accustomed to do in the summer months. The RCWU leaders were worried to the point where they held a secret ballot vote on May 29 so that it could not be said that the camp workers were striking against their will. The question on the ballot was, "Are you in favour of carrying on the relief camp strike?" There were 923 votes cast: 637 yes, 270 no, and sixteen spoiled ballots.[56] While the result indicated two-thirds in favour of continuing the strike, the number of votes cast indicates that several hundred had not voted. Many had applied for reinstatement and many more had boarded freights for other destinations. Some of the men still in Vancouver who had not voted must have declined to do so from a feeling that the strike was defeated. A Vancouver city police undercover agent made an assessment of the situation which may be fairly accurate.

> This is 70 per cent in favour of carrying on the struggle, here in Vancouver. Of course, this was no surprise as the Strikers are still as Militant as ever, but afraid of the Police. Fully 400 did not vote and also about 200 or 300 have left town on the freights, in the last few nights.[57]

The strike leadership appears to have concluded that, even with the favourable vote, it would be very difficult to hold the strike together for much longer in Vancouver. Ronald Liversedge, in his *Recollections of the On-to-Ottawa Trek*, describes the problem which faced the strikers.

> A feeling of apathy was beginning to be felt amongst the camp strikers; the strain of the long struggle was beginning to be felt, and we could not ignore the fact that we were losing many of our members. It was in this atmosphere that a special night meeting of the central strike committee was called to discuss the situation.[58]

It was at this meeting, held on the night of May 29, that the idea of a mass trek to Ottawa by freight train seems to have been born. Liversedge states, and other sources seem to bear this out, that it originated as a spontaneous suggestion from an unnamed member of the Strike Committee.[59] The proposal was discussed and endorsed by the Strike Committee and recommended to a mass meeting of the strikers on May 30.

The proposal to undertake the On-to-Ottawa Trek was endorsed by the mass meeting of May 30. Steve Broder, who attended the meeting, recalled the event years later.

> Immediately the whole place caught fire. There was tremendous enthusiasm and speaker after speaker got up there to talk about how the thing could be organized and get under way. The enthusiasm was tremendous.[60]

Monday, June 3, was set as the departure date for the journey to Ottawa. The meeting also sent a delegation to Mayor McGeer with the following requests: (1) Relief for the men until their departure for Ottawa; (2) Permission to hold a tag day on Saturday, June 1, to raise money for the trip to Ottawa; (3) Financing an advance delegation of three representatives of the strikers to Ottawa to negotiate with the federal government. McGeer, by now in an ugly mood, rejected all three requests and was reported by the press to have denounced the strikers.

> He declared that by their association with Communists, nuisance parades and assaults on police they had forfeited any right to the City's assistance.[61]

An illegal tag day was held on June 1 in any event and was reported to have netted $1510 despite the arrest of about twenty people.[62] A picnic for the camp workers was held in Stanley Park on June 2, with women sympathizers supplying the food.

The strikers left Vancouver as scheduled on June 3 in two groups of men; they were to meet at Kamloops where they would stay for two days before proceeding eastward. About 700 left on a CPR freight at 8:30 p.m. and were followed by another 200 who boarded a CNR freight about midnight.[63] Another group estimated at 300-400 left Vancouver in the evening of June 4 to join the trek at Golden to the east of Kamloops.

The Vancouver *Province* of June 4 carried a description of the main contingent leaving the Vancouver freight yards.

> As the locomotive of the ninety car train started its deep coughing in an endeavour to put into motion its huge load there was a

cheer from its horde of uninvited passengers, who clung to the tops of the cars like swarming bees. The cheer was answered by the large crowd, composed of all classes of Vancouver citizenry, who lined the right-of-way from the depot east to Heatly Avenue.

No attempts were made by railway police or any other police force to prevent the men from boarding the freights and moving eastward. CPR train crews, in fact, facilitated the boarding of trains and CPR officials kept authorities informed of the estimated number and the behaviour of the trekkers.[65] That both Premier Pattullo and Mayor McGeer would be glad to see the trekkers leave Vancouver had long been obvious. The strike leaders were correct in assuming there would be no opposition to their departure from the city and the province.

The federal government did not attempt to convince British Columbia that they should try to prevent the illegal boarding of trains. In view of the impending Longshoremen's strike, which began on June 6, they probably preferred to have the strikers out of Vancouver even if it meant merely postponing a showdown. Before the trek got underway, DND officials also appear to have been working under the assumption that the whole scheme was impractical and merely a last ditch attempt by RCWU leaders to minimize the political impact of a total defeat of the strike.[66] General Ashton reported to McNaughton on June 1 that this was the general opinion in Vancouver. "Impression is general that proposed march on Ottawa possibly announced to save faces of organizers and give excuse for breaking up strike." If the impression was correct the trek would eventually disintegrate of its own accord and spare the authorities a confrontation which might involve bloodshed and negative political consequences for the government.

In his *Recollections of the On-to-Ottawa Trek* Ronald Liversedge presents an assessment of opinion in Vancouver which is remarkably similar to the perception which General Ashton reported to Ottawa.

It was felt by the camp workers that the secret majority opinion of the people of Vancouver (including our friends) was that we had put up a great struggle, but that we were at last defeated and that our ranks would melt away soon after leaving Vancouver.[67]

If this was a correct reading of the general opinion, the country was soon to discover that, as Liversedge was to write years later, "Public opinion was never in greater error..."[68]

Footnotes

1. Public Archives of Canada (PAC), *McNaughton Papers,* Vol. 61, File 380 (B), M.D. 11 to CGS, April 24, 1935. Also Ben Swankey and Jean Evans Sheils, *Work and Wages: A Semi-Documentary Account of the Life and Times of Arthur H. (Slim) Evans, 1890-1944* (Vancouver: Trade Union Research Bureau, 1977), p. 91.
2. *McNaughton Papers,* (B), M.D. 11 to CGS, April 24, 1935.
3. Vancouver *News Herald,* quoted in Swankey and Sheils, *op. cit.,* p. 90.
4. Bob Bouchette, "The Events Leading up to the Riot," Vancouver *Sun,* April 24, 1935.
5. Ottawa *Citizen,* April 25, 1935.
6. *McNaughton Papers,* Vol. 61, File 380 (B), T. Forkin to Prime Minister Bennett, April 25, 1935.
7. Swankey and Sheils, *op. cit.,* p. 93.
8. Vancouver City Police Department Report CID Branch, April 25, 1935. Report contained in Victor Hoar (ed.), *Recollections of the On-to-Ottawa Trek* by Ronald Liversedge (Toronto: McClelland and Stewart, 1973), p. 153.
9. Swankey and Sheils, *op. cit.,* p. 94.
10. *McNaughton Papers,* Vol. 61, File 380 (B), M.D. 11 to CGS, April 30, 1935.
11. *Ibid.*
12. *Ibid.,* Vol. 62, File 380 (B), M.D. 22 to CGS, April 30, 1935.
13. PAC, *Bennett Papers,* p. 495673, Mrs. W.T. Robinson (Correspondence Secretary), WCTU to Bennett, March 23, 1935.
14. *Ibid.,* pp. 495587-8, Rolston to Bennett, April 25, 1935.
15. *Ibid.,* pp. 496380, 496366, 495784-85, 495792, 495794-5, 495802, 495808-09.
16. The Price Spreads Commission had been looking into abuses related to chain retail stores. Stevens had, through the Commission, established a reputation as a crusader for fair prices and improved labour conditions. He split with Bennett when the government caved in to pressure from the big retail chains.
17. *Bennett Papers,* pp. 496383-85, H.H. Stevens to Perley, April 30, 1935.
18. *Ibid.*
19. *Idid.,* p. 496401, Lyon to Perley, May 2, 2935.
20. *Ibid.,* p. 495763, Wilkinson to Merriam, April 28, 1935.
21. *Ibid.,* p. 496432, Schofield to Bennett, May 11, 1935.
22. *Ibid.,* pp. 496370-74, Marshal to Bennett, April 29, 1935.
23. *Ibid.*
24. *Ibid.*
25. *McNaughton Papers,* Vol. 61, File 380 (B), Memorandum by McNaughton on telephone conversation with Ashton, April 27, 1935.
26. *Bennett Papers,* p. 495791, text of public statement by Perley.

27. *Ibid.*
28. Ottawa *Citizen,* April 27, 1935.
29. Swankey and Sheils, *op. cit.,* p. 94.
30. Vancouver City Police Department, Foster to McGeer, May 2, 1935. Contained in Hoar, *op. cit.,* p. 157.
31. Vancouver City Police Department, Unaddressed and unsigned memorandum, May 1, 1935. Contained in Hoar, *op. cit.,* p. 159.
32. *McNaughton Papers,* File 359 (Vol. IV). Also see Swankey and Sheils, *op. cit.,* p. 94.
33. Dr. Lyle Telford, provincial CCF leader, and some of his associates tended to be weak in their support. The same was true of many local and most national TLC leaders.
34. *Bennett Papers,* Mayor McGeer to Sir George Perley, May 14, 1935. Also cited in Hoar, *op.cit.,* p. 161.
35. VCPD, an addressed and unsigned memorandum, May 12, 1935. Cited in Hoar, *op. cit.,* p. 160.
36. Hoar, *op. cit.,* p. 160; Swankey and Shiels, *op. cit.,* p. 95.
37. Montreal *Gazette,* May 11, 1935.
38. VCPD, unaddressed and unsigned memorandum, May 12, 1935. Cited in Hoar, *op. cit.,* p. 160.
39. Strikers' leaflet, reproduced in Swankey and Sheils, *op. cit.,* p. 96.
40. *Ibid.*
41. McGeer to Bennett, May 16, 1935. Cited in Regina Riot Inquiry Commission (RRIC) Report, pp. 84-85, and cited again in Hoar, *op. cit.,* p. l62.
42. The occupation of the Vancouver City Museum is described in 76-83, and in Hoar, *op. cit.*; Swankey and Sheils, *op. cit.,* pp. 97-98.
43. Hoar, *op. cit.,* pp. 76-83.
44. *McNaughton Papers,* File 380 (B), McNaughton memorandum on telephone conversation with Ashton, May 19, 1935.
45. *Ibid.,* File 380 (B), M.D. 11 to CGS, May 23, 1935 and Swankey and Sheils, *op. cit.,* p. 99.
46. Swankey and Sheils, *op. cit.,* pp. 99-100.
47. *McNaughton Papers,* Vol. 58, clipping from Montreal *Daily Star,* May 27, 1935.
48. Vancouver *Province*, May 28, 1935.
49. *McNaughton Papers,* File 380 (B), Sloan to McNaughton, not dated, repeated in telegram from McNaughton to Ashton, May 28, 1935.
50. *McNaughton Papers,* File 380 (B), M.D. 11 to CGS, May 29, 1935.
51. *Ibid.*
52. *Ibid.,* File 380 (B), Ashton to McNaughton, May 29, 1935 and May 31, 1935. Also unaddressed and unsigned memorandum, May 29, 1935, in VCPD, cited in Hoar, *op. cit.,* pp. 169-71. This police undercover agent saw the strike as beaten and nearly over. He stated that "... the large Police showing and the knowledge that the police were ready for business was the final factor."

53. Unaddressed and unsigned memorandum, May 28, 1935, in VCPD, cited in Hoar, *op. cit.,* pp. 169-171.
54. Hoar, *op. cit.,* p. XVII.
55. Unaddressed and unsigned memorandum, May 29, 1935, in VCPD, cited in Hoar, *op. cit.,* pp. 169-71.
56. *McNaughton Papers,* File 380 (B), M.D. 11 to CGS, May 31, 1935.
57. Unaddressed and unsigned memorandum, May 30, 1935, VCPD, cited in Hoar, *op. cit.,* pp. 171-73.
58. Hoar, *op. cit.,* p. 83.
59. Hoar, *op. cit.,* pp. 83-84. Arthur Evans has generally been credited with conceiving the idea of the On-to-Ottawa Trek, perhaps because it was he who introduced the proposal to the mass meeting of strikers which endorsed it (Swankey and Sheils, p. 104). Stan Lowe claims that it was first talked about at a meeting of Communist Party members (Swankey and Sheils, p. 104). While this could have been the case it does appear that the Communist Party leadership neither discussed or even favoured the idea at first. The leadership of the Workers' Unity League at first instructed Evans that he was to proceed with the Trek only to Golden, British Columbia, and then return to perform organizing duties in Vancouver (Swankey and Sheils, p. 112). He and others convinced them to reverse this decision and Evans resumed the leadership of the Trek. Bob Kerr, an activist at the time, claims that the Communists and WUL leadership in Vancouver had serious doubts about the Trek. "The Central Committee [presumably of either the Communist Party or the WUL] had some doubts about the trek. They expected that the authorities would try to get them on a siding, isolate them and surround them with the RCMP and the army. He came back from Golden and he convinced them to endorse it." Swankey and Sheils, p. 289.
60. Swankey and Sheils, *op. cit.,* p. 106.
61. Vancouver *Province,* May 30, 1935.
62. *Ibid.,* June 3, 1935.
63. *McNaughton Papers,* File 380 (B), M.D. 11 to CGS, June 5, 1935.
64. *Ibid.*
65. *McNaughton Papers,* File 380 (B), M.D. 13 to Adjutant-General, June 6, 1935. Also see Swankey and Sheils, p. 110.
66. *Ibid.,* File 380 (B), M.D. 11 to CGS, June 1, 1935.
67. Hoar, *op. cit.,* p. 85.
68. *Ibid.*

CHAPTER VIII

A Migration Unique in the History of Canada

Those officials from the Department of National Defence and others who assumed that the On-to-Ottawa Trek would soon fall apart were to be proven wrong very quickly. From the time the relief camp strikers left Vancouver until they were disbanded in Regina after the Regina Riot, only once does there appear to have been a danger of major defections from their ranks due to discouragement and demoralization: when they reached Kamloops on June 4. It appears that the advance publicity committee had done a poor job of preparing the public for the arrival of the Trek: adequate arrangements had not been made for food and shelter and the population of Kamloops seemed uninterested in the event.

Ronald Liversedge describes the mood of the men, the desire to disband the Trek and travel on their own or in small groups.

> It was here that the breaking point was just about reached by some of the men, and the first time since the strike started that I had seen our self-discipline thrown to the winds. Some of the men were advocating leaving the trek, stating that if it was going to be like this that we might be dead before we reached Calgary.
>
> Many thought they could live and eat better on their own or in small groups. There was argument and debate. This was not an organized attempt to disrupt the trek. Every one of the men had been living a tense life for the past three months, a life of constant activity, picketing, demonstrating, door to door canvassing, fighting with the police, many of them spending some time in jail, always hungry, and for many, the floor of our meeting

halls had been their nightly couch. This outburst in Kamloops, then, was the culmination of all that had gone before.[1]

This questioning of the viability of the Trek was, according to Liversedge, overcome by arguments put forth by Arthur Evans, who had been chosen as Leader of the expedition.[2]

> Evans said that he was sure that this would be our worst experience. It was our first port of call, and the people were not yet experienced in meeting such a big bunch, but they would soon catch on. The people had not yet realized the possibility of such a movement, but they would very quickly, and then our worst difficulties would be over.[3]

Evans also assured the strikers that they could rest up, replenish their resources, and pick up more recruits from the unemployed when they reached Calgary.

The morale of the trekkers improved when they were able to collect enough food to tide them over in Kamloops and when they held a public meeting which was reasonably well attended. The reception was much better at Golden, near the Kicking Horse Pass. Arthur Evans had arrived in Golden in advance and arranged with Mrs. Sorley, a local farm woman, to prepare food and a reception for the main body of men. Mrs. Sorley formed a joint committee of the local Workers' Protective Association and the CCF. They collected food and cooking equipment from farmers and townspeople and arranged for the use of the local tourist park.

The trekkers arrived in Golden on the morning of June 6 and were welcomed by a committee who led them to the tourist park. Ronald Liversedge describes the tremendous reception awaiting the tired trekkers in his *Recollections of the On-to-Ottawa Trek*:

> We very soon marched on to a large expanse of park-like land, richly grassed, with large shade trees scattered here and there. A truly sylvan setting, but what was more to the point, under a half dozen of those hugh shade trees were cooking fires, and suspended over the fires were various kinds of make-shift cooking vessels full to the brims, with simmering, bubbling, thick, heavenly-smelling beef stew. The cooking pots were make-shift because they had to be big. Over one fire (and this is the gospel truth) was suspended a full size bathtub, also full to the brim with beef stew. There were long trestle tables with thousands of slices of

golden crusted bread. Around each fire were just two or three quiet, smiling women, salting, peppering and tasting.

It was incredible, it was heartwarming, it was beautiful.

The column of men halted, a thunderous cheer arose, and the men broke ranks and rushed over to embrace those quiet, smiling, wonderful women of Golden. That little whitehaired woman had, with the aid of our advance committee, mobilized the farmers in that valley of Golden. With only twenty-four hours to work on, they had procured here a calf, there a quarter of beef, there potatoes, there carrots, turnips, onions, all in huge quantities, set all the women to baking bread, collecting cooking utensils, plates and mugs, with the end result which welcomed us on our arrival. All this had been accomplished with an absence of fuss and bother.

The people of Golden knew about us, and our struggles; they knew about the relief camps. Their welcome of us was the welcome of pioneers, heartfelt, deep, and sincere. Golden stood out in the memory of the trekkers as the most restful, tranquil episode of the whole trek.

Quickly the camp workers jumped in to relieve the men and women who had worked so hard to greet us. Squads of cooks, waiters, fire tenders, and water carriers were soon organized, and before long dinner was served. That never-to-be-forgotten meal! The weather was ideal, the outdoor site was superb, and our hosts were the salt of the earth.

During the meal many farmers and their wives and children came into the park, and joined the various groups of men for dinner. There was good conversation. We told of the slave camps, our long strike in Vancouver, and our hope for negotiations with the Dominion Government.

We learned that we were already nationwide news, with every radio news broadcast following our trip east.

The trekkers spent one day and a night at Golden and then proceeded to Calgary, arriving on the evening of June 7. By this time the news about the Trek had spread so thoroughly throughout the country that sympathizers were well organized to lend assistance. There seemed little doubt that the Trek would remain intact.

There were a number of reasons for the fact that the trekkers were able to hold themselves together, increase in numbers, and maintain public support as they moved across the country. Their highly developed organizational structure and tight discipline came from the relief camps and from their Vancouver experiences. They were organized into groups of twelve, each with a group leader.

Liversedge describes the advantages of the group system of organization.

> There were many advantages to this type of organization one of the main ones being that it was practically foolproof against the planting of provocateurs in our ranks. The group always sat together at meetings, marched together in parades, worked together on strike duties, and came to spend their leisure time together. The men got to know each other, and to trust each other in emergencies and there was a loyalty and *esprit de corps* built up in the groups.[4]

Then there was the "division." There were three divisions during the Vancouver strike—each with a chairman, secretary, marshals, and other officers who made up a sort of unofficial steering committee. There was also a Central Strike Committee which oversaw the whole strike.

The organizational structure developed in Vancouver was kept intact for the Trek. The Central Strike Committee was renamed the On-to-Ottawa Committee and given responsibility for overseeing arrangements and strategy for the whole expedition. New recruits were integrated into the existing structures and a fourth division was added in Calgary.

Orderliness, discipline, and proper deportment were emphasized even more on the Trek than they had been in Vancouver. No one was allowed to join the Trek unless he agreed to follow discipline. Arthur Evans always emphasized this when he discussed the Trek experience.

> I pointed out that we would sooner have quality than quantity, that the main thing that would assist us in getting our grievances before the government would be the support that we would receive from the public enroute, and that the only way this could be obtained would be by maintaining ourselves in a well organized and disciplined manner.[5]

This discipline and orderliness was frequently commented upon by the press and by DND officials in their reports to National Defence Headquarters. The District Officer Commanding for Military District 13 (Alberta and Eastern British Columbia) reported to the Adjutant-General, "No misbehaviour, report conduct on railway good, railway officials report no trouble to date."[6] The Officer

Commanding in Regina made similar comments. "Excellent organization and a good discipline exert favourable impression on citizens."[7]

Another important element in the organization and success of the Trek was that the RCWU and the WUL had numerous contacts in the large cities and many of the smaller towns and cities. These included, in addition to supporters of the WUL and the Communist Party, a fairly broad left-wing community associated with such organizations as the Canadian Labour Defence League and ethnic associations like the Ukrainian Farmer-Labour Temple Association. There were also many sympathizers in the CCF and the farm organizations. These organizations and individuals were invaluable in publicizing the demands of the Trek, establishing support committees in the cities along the route, and providing food, meeting halls, printing facilities, and money.

The leaders of the Trek were able to make maximum use of their extensive organizational contacts and expand upon them because of their political astuteness and willingness to adapt flexible tactics. They attempted to broaden their base of support by concentrating their publicity on the specific grievances and demands of the unemployed rather than calling for immediate revolutionary changes which people knew were not possible in Canada in 1935.

The population of the Prairies was ripe for receiving the trekkers. The destitution of the farmers and working people was such that the Bennett government had become the most unpopular regime in living memory. And on the provincial level the Conservatives had been almost obliterated as a political force. By 1935 they barely existed in Alberta and Saskatchewan and were weak in Manitoba. The population was in a restive move.

Perhaps the most important thing that the Trek had going for it was that the very audacity of the expedition appealed to the imagination of the public. While all levels of government and the more conservative elements of the population may have been apprehensive about what appeared to be a defiance of constituted authority, a broad cross section of people who had grievances against the system could identify with the causes of the trekkers and their attempt to take their demands to the doorstep of the Ottawa government.

The Trek also appealed to the imagination of journalists. The event became an important news story. The article in the Vancouver *Province* describing the Trek's departure from Vancouver called it "a migration unique in the history of Canada."[8] The tone of the article was sympathetic to the trekkers with considerable emphasis on the youth of the participants. "Canadian youth was sending the delegation to Ottawa to demand a place in the country's society. It was a delegation of youth. Few of the mass contingent were more than 30."[9] At least one reporter, James Kingsbury of the Toronto *Star*, accompanied the trekkers from Vancouver, and his reports, which were generally favourable to the trekkers, were carried in many Canadian newspapers.

The Trek was also attracting interest in the House of Commons. Several questions had been asked by opposition M.P.'s. and there had been brief discussion around the situation in B.C. both before and after the walkout of April 4. Members had become more concerned as tension mounted in late May and there was some opposition pressure, particularly from CCF members, for an emergency debate on the situation. On May 21 Angus MacInnis asked Prime Minister Bennett about reports in the Ottawa *Journal* that the federal government was considering intervention in the B.C. situation. Bennett replied that the federal government would intervene only upon provincial request.

> for until that is done any action on the part of the dominion would be wholly illegal and would be a compromising of our position with those who may themselves be violating the law.[10]

Bennett was to maintain this line until the federal decision to stop the Trek and then go back on his own statements and intervene in Regina against the wishes of the Saskatchewan government.

Bennett used the same reasoning in refusing an emergency debate requested by MacInnis on May 22.[11] Nor was there debate when MacInnis tabled a petition from British Columbia signed by 10,800 people requesting amendments to the Elections Act to guarantee relief camp workers the right to vote.[12]

Once the Trek was underway the prime minister was called upon to be specific about the federal attitude to the expedition. Premier R.C. Reid of Alberta made an unofficial request on June 4 and another on June 6 that the federal authorities intervene to prevent the Trek from reaching Alberta. Premier John Bracken of Manitoba was to make a similar request in respect to his province on June 10. Bennett refused to intervene unless *officially* requested to do so by the province or provinces concerned. The prime minister announced to the House that illegal trespassing on CNR and CPR property was a matter to be dealt with by the railways and the provincial governments.

A number of telegrams have been received apprehending difficulties, but we have told them that when complaints have been made against trespassers, at the request of the provincial authorities we are ready to render such assistance as may be within our power and as they may require. [13]

Bennett's excuse for not negotiating with the trekkers was that they were associated with communists.

I need hardly say that there are several well known communistic societies under varying names; they have sought to embroil the government in some discussion in respect to these matters, and we have declined to enter into any discussion with them. [14]

This was an obvious attempt to deny the legitimacy of the RCWU or any similar organization speaking on behalf of the organized unemployed. It was ironic in that the Bennett government itself had long since lost credibility and was coming dangerously close to losing actual legitimacy in the eyes of a great many people across Canada.

Until June 11 Bennett held firm to his position. While the Trek was still in Alberta, however, the federal authorities decided to stop it in Saskatchewan. Events surrounding the trekkers' stay in Calgary were probably what convinced Bennett and his ministers that the Trek was not going to disintegrate of its own accord. On the contrary, it was picking up support rapidly and had already caught the public imagination. By the time the trekkers left Calgary they were already on their way to creating a modern popular legend. And they had not yet even reached Winnipeg—the historic centre of Prairie radicalism.

The trekkers had planned their activities in Calgary very well. An advance party of leaders had set up headquarters in the Calgary Labour Temple, formed committees of local supporters, and even held one public meeting before the arrival of the trekkers. Mayor Davison agreed that the men could be housed in the grandstand building at the exhibition grounds but refused to supply meal tickets or allow a tag day. Davison's strategy was apparently to make some concessions to minimize the possibility of trouble but to refuse relief in the hope that the trekkers would make their stay in Calgary as brief as possible.

Local supporters did a good job of providing advance publicity for Calgary events. A leaflet announced that the trekkers would be in Calgary three days, declared the purpose of the Trek to be the abolition of the relief camps, announced the time and place of a picnic in support of the camp workers, and appealed for public moral and financial support. "We invite all political, economic, cultural and church organizations to give us their support in our just fight for the abolition of the present relief camp system."[15] There was also a broadcast on radio station CFAC the evening the trekkers arrived in the city.

The leaflet and broadcast were shrewd political moves by the Trek strategists. They provided accurate information about the purposes of the Trek, appealed for support, and revealed that the men would not be in the city for long. It was made clear to the public that the Trekkers' demands were reasonable despite what government authorities might claim.

With public support established, the trekkers were in a position to carry out what had to be done. When the mayor refused to provide public relief or allow a tag day the tactics of the strikers were adjusted to get both. They held an illegal tag day and collected over $1500.[16] They also obtained donations of food and clothing from Calgary supporters.

The strikers obtained public relief by using the type of audacious tactics for which they had become known in Vancouver, They interviewed Mayor Davison on the morning of June 8 in another attempt to obtain municipal relief but were again turned down and told that relief for people from outside Calgary was either a provincial or a federal responsibility. A group of strikers accompanied by local supporters then went to the Provincial Relief Office and sent in a delegation to interview A.A. McKenzie, Provincial Relief Officer.[17]

McKenzie had already despatched a telegram to Harry Hereford, Commissioner of Unemployment Relief in Ottawa, informing him that the men would be asking for relief and requesting instructions. A member of the delegation named MacLeod, upon being shown the telegram, is reported to have declared, "No, that will not do. You will send a wire demanding that we be fed and sheltered. You send another wire and tell them that we demand assistance and that you will be prepared to give this on their approval. Until this is done you might as well know that the men can go without food just as long as you can in this office."[18] The strikers and their supporters then proceeded to barricade the Relief Office and place pickets at every exit. Left inside the office and more or less imprisoned were McKenzie, a number of other relief officials, and Dr. Stanley, Conservative M.P. for Calgary East who had been conferring with McKenzie and others at the time.

McKenzie telephoned the required messages to the telegraph office and also got in touch with provincial government officials in Edmonton. The matter was finally settled and what became known as the "siege" of the Provincial Relief Office was ended when the government of Alberta instructed the Calgary municipal authorities to provide $600 worth of meal tickets for the trekkers.[19] The "siege" had lasted from 11 a.m. to 2:35 in the afternoon.

The events at the Relief Office had alarmed provincial officials and local military officials. Lord Strathcona's Horse was put on the alert while the "siege" was still in progress.[20] A.A. McKenzie was shaken up by the experience and wired his concern to federal Labour Minister Gordon.

> Regarding British Columbia single men. A dangerous revolutionary army intimidating and defying provincial and municipal governments by threats and actually holding officials as hostage until demands met. Their success having a far reaching effect that may be difficult to control.[21]

The local military expressed similar concerns. In reporting to Ottawa on the Calgary picnic and public rally held on June 9 the local Officer Commanding warned that actions such as the "siege" might occur in the future. "Speaker today said public militant action will be taken by men any time demands not acceded to."[22] He claimed in the same communication to have information from a "reliable source" that the Trek had revolutionary implications, though he did not define what he meant by "revolutionary." "Talk amongst men this is revolutionary movement, large numbers expected to join at Winnipeg and Toronto."[23]

The possibility of widespread civil disobedience alarmed the authorities—what particularly worried them was that acts of civil disobedience were receiving considerable support from the public and even from some newspapers. The Calgary *Albertan* was a strong supporter of the Trek and one of Bennett's supporters sent him several editorial clippings with a note to the effect he thought they represented public opinion. One editorial discussed the charge that the Trek was organized and led by communists and concluded that, since the trekkers' demands were reasonable, the issue was not very relevant. "To be quite frank, we don't care very much."[24]

Another *Albertan* editorial entitled "What These Marchers Want" chastised A.A. McKenzie for claiming that the Trek resembled an invading army rather than a peaceful march.

> We will not disagree that fundamentally the pilgrimage is a series of riots inasmuch as the authorities could not intervene or chose not to at one place today and another place tomorrow. That is to say they are bloodless riots which amuse rather than inconvenience the townsmen who see them staged.[25]

The editorial also dismissed McKenzie's protests at having been locked in the Relief Office for several hours.

> He might have been the victim of a less disciplined, less organized body of men. But he was not; he really was co-victim with them of a Government at Ottawa which has deferred men's hopes—all our hopes—so often, promised us so much and given us so little that at length the chief sufferers have determined to go to Ottawa and ask the Prime Minister himself what he proposed to do about it.[26]

The trekkers were urged to go on to Ottawa and not take no for an answer.

The trekkers left Calgary on the night of June 10 and took with them several hundred new recruits, many of whom had come on a freight from Edmonton. They were single unemployed men who had been cut off relief for refusing to go to the camps. By now it was clear beyond a doubt that, far from disintegrating, the Trek would probably number many thousands by the time it reached Ottawa. It was also clear that the credibility of the Bennett government had reached a new low and many people were even beginning to question the very legitimacy of the government and the state. The Bennett regime would at last have to negotiate in good faith or stop the Trek by a show of force and the risk of bloodshed.

It was on June 11, while the trekkers were still in Medicine Hat, that the federal government decided to stop the Trek when it reached Regina. They did so without consulting with and against the wishes of the government of Saskatchewan. Premier Gardiner was first informed of the decision by Assistant Commissioner Wood of the RCMP.[27] This represented a reversal of previous federal policy, stated on innumerable occasions in the House of Commons and in communications to authorities in B.C., Alberta and Manitoba, that Ottawa would act only upon official provincial request.

The federal government claimed it was responding to a request from the railways for assistance to prevent trespassing on their trains and since the Railway Act was federal it was under their jurisdiction. But it was obvious that the railways had been set up by the federal government to make such a request.[28] Normally they would have first requested provincial assistance since law enforcement came under their jurisdiction. And previously the railways had been co-operating fully with the trekkers. From the point of view of the railways the trekkers were no more of an inconvenience by June 11 than they had been from the beginning.

The federal government had decided that Regina was a convenient place to stop the Trek. There was a sizable RCMP contingent in the city in addition to the personnel at the RCMP training depot. There were also facilities for the accommodation of reinforcements. Also, the next major centre was Winnipeg, a large city with a radical tradition and a large left-wing movement where the trekkers could be expected to obtain both massive public support and many recruits. Regina was smaller and did not have a large labour movement. But the political atmosphere in Regina and Saskatchewan proved to be anything but tame. The decision to stop the Trek was bitterly opposed by the Liberal government, the CCF official opposition, the most influential newspapers, and most major mass organizations. Premier Gardiner had previously made arrangements to provide the trekkers with meals and accommodation at provincial expense while they were in Saskatchewan. There appeared to be no reason for any trouble, let alone a major confrontation with the trekkers during their brief stay in the province.

When the Bennett government upset his plans without so much as consulting him, Gardiner was enraged and said so publicly. He was backed up by the official opposition and the public. The Bennett government had set itself up for a major showdown, not only with the trekkers but also with the province.

Footnotes

1. Victor Hoar (ed.), *Recollections of the On-to-Ottawa Trek* by Ronald Liversedge (McClelland and Stewart Ltd., 1973), p. 87.
2. Ben Swankey and Jean Evans Sheils, *Work and Wages: A Semi-Documentary Account of the Life and Times of Arthur H. (Slim) Evans, 1890-1944* (Vancouver Trade Union Research Bureau, 1977), p. 109. Evans returned from Golden to Vancouver on orders from the Workers' Unity League and was temporarily replaced as Trek leader by William Black. He rejoined the expedition as leader at Medicine Hat.
3. Hoar, *op. cit.*, p. 87.
4. *Ibid.*, p. 67.

5. Swankey and Sheils, *op. cit.,* p. 104.
6. Public Archives of Canada (PAC), *McNaughton Papers,* File 380 (B), M.D. 13 to A.G., June 6, 1935.
7. *Ibid.,* File 380 (B).
8. Vancouver *Province,* article cited in Swankey and Sheils, *op. cit.,* p. 107.
9. *Ibid.*
10. House of Commons *Debates,* 1935 Version, Vol. III, pp. 2921-22, May 21, 1935.
11. *Ibid.*
12. *Ibid.,* p. 3141, May 29, 1935.
13. *Ibid.,* p. 3396, June 7, 1935.
14. *Ibid.*
15. Leaflet distributed by Trek supporters in Calgary, copy contained in Swankey and Sheils, *op. cit.,* p. 111.
16. *McNaughton Papers,* Vol. 61, File 380 (B), M.D. 13 to A.G., June 9, 1935.
17. The description of the events which followed is contained in the *McNaughton Papers,* Vol. 61, File 380 (B), M.D. 13 to A.G. June 8, 9 and 10, 1935 and in the *Regina Riot Inquiry Report* (RRIC), pp. 58-60, cited in Hoar, *op. cit.,* p. 175.
18. RRIC *Report,* pp. 58-60, also cited in Hoar, *op. cit.,* pp. 175-76.
19. *McNaughton Papers,* Vol. 61, File 380 (B), M.D. 13 to A.G., June 9, 1935.
20. *McNaughton Papers,* Vol. 61, File 380 (B), M.D. 13 to A.G., June 8, 1935.
21. *Bennett Papers,* p. 496566, A. A. McKenzie to Gordon, June 11, 1935.
22. *McNaughton Papers,* Vol. 62, File 380 (B), M.D. 13 to A.G., June 9, 1935.
23. *Ibid.*
24. Public Archives of Canada (PAC), *Bennett Papers,* p. 495960, clipping from Calgary *Albertan,* June 13, 1935.
25. *Ibid.*
26. *Ibid.*
27. Gardiner testimony at the RRIC, cited in Swankey and Sheils, *op. cit.*
28. RRIC *Report,* p. 116, "Cunningham Submission," pp. 18-22. The railways did not even request provincial assistance until June 12, one day after the federal government decided to stop the Trek. In fact Gardiner was first informed that such a request would be made in a telegram from Prime Minister Bennett. (RRIC *Report,* p. 90, Bennett to Gardiner, June 12, 1935). The requests from the two railways arrived later the same day.

CHAPTER IX
Stalemate in Regina and Confrontation in Ottawa

The main body of trekkers arrived in Saskatchewan on June 12. They had been preceded by advance delegations who had made agreements with municipal and provincial officials for accommodation and meal tickets at provincial expense. They had also established local support committees to influence public opinion and collect money and other material assistance.

The strikers received more assistance here than they had in either B.C. or Alberta. Their local support committees were also well organized and they benefitted from a press which was generally hostile to the federal government.

The trekkers arrived in Swift Current about noon on their first day in the province and were met by a committee which directed them to restaurants taking government supplied meal tickets. A local unemployed association sponsored a public meeting at the athletic grounds. The Trek reached Moose Jaw that same evening and remained there the following day. The men were again given meal tickets and accommodated at the city sports ground. Local support groups sponsored meetings to inform the public of the strikers' demands. In his address to one of the gatherings, Arthur Evans reported on a meeting he and an advance delegation had held with Premier Gardiner earlier in the day. Gardiner had informed them of provincial plans for feeding and housing the trekkers while they were in Regina; the delegation had informed the premier that they would be in Regina for two or three days. Several speakers at the Moose Jaw meetings also declared that the Trek would proceed to Ottawa as planned. [1] It was clear that both the trekkers and the provincial government were determined the Trek would not be stopped in Regina regardless of federal determination to the contrary.

The strikers arrived in Regina in the early morning of June 14. They now numbered between 1500 and 1800—reinforcements which had been added in Alberta, Swift Current, and Moose Jaw. They hoped that several hundred more would join them in Regina from the big camp at Dundurn near Saskatoon. Regina was well organized. In addition to the official arrangements for food and shelter, the Citizen's Emergency Relief Committee had been formed to arrange moral and material support. Public sympathy was guaranteed by the fact that both the provincial Liberal government and the CCF opposition had already declared themselves against the federal intervention, and the politicians were backed up by most mass organizations and the press.

The federal authorities were well aware of the mood in Saskatchewan. Brigadier Boak, the local District Officer Commanding, reported to Ottawa on June 14 and again the next day that provincial and municipal officials and public opinion were all sympathetic to the strikers.[2] Identical reports were received by the federal department of labour from their Regina representatives on June 15.[3]

Bennett was also informed by prominent Saskatchewan Conservatives that public opinion was with the trekkers and that some concessions would be necessary if a violent clash was to be avoided.

> Vancouver Relief Camp marchers paraded Regina today in considerable strength. Vicious propaganda Liberal leader and press coupled with orderly conduct and apparent unity of marchers strongly influenced public sympathy in their favour. Fear that subversive leaders may lead their men into conflict with authority. Situation really full of dynamite. Strongly recommend utmost effort to bring about amicable arrangement to end further progress of march eastward. Marching slogan is "We want work and wages." Suggest offer work in mines or road building British Columbia if possible or in alternative that four or five leaders be granted free conduct to Ottawa to interview you or your colleagues, others to be returned to British Columbia camps forthwith to await result of interview.[4]

The military, labour officials and the Conservatives were accurate in their assessment. The first night in Regina, a public meeting at the exhibition stadium attracted 6000 people and representatives of fourteen organizations spoke from the platform.[5] Speakers included M.J. Coldwell, provincial CCF leader; Reverend John Mutch of Knox United Church; C.B. McDaniels from the Catholic Church;

D. Fisher, President of the Regina Trades and Labour Council; T.G. McManus of the Communist Party, and Arthur Evans on behalf of the RCWU and the Trek.

Coldwell pledged the support of the Saskatchewan CCF to what he described as the "army of forgotten youth" and asserted that they had earned the respect of the population in the cities through which they had passed.[6] McDaniels said that the "battalion of unwanted youth" was justified "if only to arouse public opinion as to conditions existing at the present time."[7] Evans assured the crowd that there would be no trouble unless the police attacked the strikers, and he declared that they would get to Ottawa despite federal intervention if they had enough public support. "But we're not in a hurry to go down and see Mr. Bennett. We want to stop at all the cities along the way and tell the citizens of the hopelessness of the relief camp situation."[8]

The meeting concluded by passing three resolutions. One was addressed to Prime Minister Bennett protesting the decision to halt the Trek. Another requested Mackenzie King and J.S. Woodsworth to protest the actions of the Bennett government in sending additional police to Regina. The third, addressed to F.N. Turnbull, Conservative M.P. for Regina, protested a statement he reportedly made to the mayor of Regina to the effect that "in the event of an emergency the militia could be called upon."[9]

The next day a tag day collected $1446 for the trekkers—the largest amount contributed during such an event in the history of Regina. On the same day the Regina *Leader-Post* carried an editorial criticizing the federal decision to intervene and chiding the Bennett government for having no constructive policy.

> The camp strikers have become a body of national importance and the Dominion Government appears to have no policy except that of force.
>
> So far as Saskatchewan is concerned the people who made it possible for the strikers to reach here by rail had better concern themselves with methods to get them out, and to get them out in the orderly fashion in which they came in.[10]

While the trekkers and their supporters were proselytizing among the public in Saskatchewan the federal authorities were busy preparing for the halting and disbandment of the Trek. They were also developing a strategy for dealing with the government of Saskatchewan. The main argument would be that the Railway Act was under federal jurisdiction and, hence, the federal government had legal authority to order the RCMP to prevent trespassing. This position was designed to get around the provincial argument that law and order was a provincial responsibility and the RCMP, being contracted as a provincial police force in Saskatchewan, should follow the orders of the attorney-general of the province in this matter as they did in enforcing the law in general. If the province objected to the federal actions they would be put in the position of appearing to shirk their responsibility for maintenance of law and order.

On June 13, RCMP Commissioner MacBrien instructed Assistant Commissioner Wood in Regina to obtain written requests from the railways to prevent trespassing. "Representatives of both railway companies here have arranged that this would be given."[11] Wood was also instructed to swear in railway police as special RCMP constables if necessary. Wood informed MacBrien on June 14 and June 15 that Acting Attorney-General J.W. Estey and Premier Gardiner had objected to the use of the RCMP in preventing trespassing by the trekkers. MacBrien instructed him to ignore Gardiner and Estey and to carry out federal orders, since railway trespassing came under federal jurisdiction and would also be within the stipulations of the federal-provincial agreement on policing. "...Agreement expressly stated Mounted Police to remain a Dominion force. Also that federal policy duties are excepted from direction of Attorney-General."[12] Assistant Commissioner Wood was also instructed to make arrangements for the reading of the Riot Act and, if he could not obtain appropriate provincial or municipal officials for this purpose, to be prepared to read it himself in his capacity as a Justice of the Peace.

On June 14 (the first full day of the Trek in Regina) the railway companies put out a joint notice to the Trek leaders, which was also distributed to the press, that trespassing would henceforth be forbidden and that the "proper authorities" had agreed to uphold the law.

> We are further instructed to inform you that if you or those associated with you further persist in unlawfully riding on the trains of either Railway Company, the proper authorities will give every assistance and use every means available to ensure that the law in this respect is observed.
>
> You are requested to disperse and return to your respective homes. If you will do this the Railway Companies will take up with the Dominion authorities the question of providing some means by which you can so return.[13]

It is clear that the "proper authorities" referred to in the notice were federal officials. Ottawa and the railways had collaborated closely to cover themselves legally. They had also prepared a case to argue politically that the province would be shirking its responsibility if it did not cooperate.

Federal authorities also made arrangements for police reinforcements and for the use of the regular army and the militia if essential. The militia posed a problem: if they were to be used without provincial request, Parliament would have to be kept sitting. McNaughton also received reports from his DOC in Regina that the militia might not be entirely reliable. "Having regard to the state of public opinion Brigadier Boak expressed doubt as to the practicability of using any local troops."[14]

Premier Gardiner was annoyed, to say the least, that matters had been taken out of his control in his own province. He was particularly alarmed at the possibility of a clash between strikers and police because of developments on Saturday, June 15. On that day the notice from the railways was carried in the newspapers; Trek leaders responded by announcing that the men would board a freight train on Monday, June 17, and calling upon the citizens of Regina to be at the railway yards as a guarantee that the police would not interfere.

Gardiner wired Bennett on June 15 in an attempt to reassert provincial authority over policing in Saskatchewan and to defuse the situation by allowing the trekkers to leave the province. Gardiner demanded that the matter be left in provincial hands and asserted the right of the province to command the RCMP in the existing circumstances.[15] Federal Justice Minister Hugh Guthrie reiterated that Ottawa had complete authority over the RCMP on the issue of railway trespassing.[16] The federal government was not prepared to back down.

What looked like the buildup to an unavoidable clash on June 17 was avoided when the federal government announced that they were sending Dr. R.J. Manion, minister of railways, and Robert Weir, minister of agriculture, to Regina with instructions to hear the grievances of the trekkers and consult with the province. They were expected to arrive in Regina on June 17. The trip was accompanied by widespread publicity and at least one newspaper, the Toronto *Globe*, made an historical reference to the federal ministers who journeyed to Winnipeg during the General Strike of 1919. This provided the Conservative press with an opportunity to portray the Bennett government as reasonable and concerned about negotiating a mutually acceptable settlement. Thus the Ottawa *Journal* waxed eloquent about the record and intentions of Bennett's regime.

> The Cabinet Ministers who have gone to Regina can show those strikers that in the matter of helping employment, as well as in the matter of caring for those who couldn't get employment, no government in the world has done more or better than the Government of Canada. No man, woman or child in this country has gone hungry or shelterless; every resource of the nation has been used to that end.
>
> It is to be sincerely hoped that those behind this march may be amenable to reason, that, after hearing the Government's case they will have some realization of the difficulties, some appreciation of its earnestness. Failing that, the country will at least know where and how to fix responsibility for possible bad consequences. [18]

The response of the Trek leaders to the news of the ministers proceeding to Regina was that they were willing to negotiate and, by implication, disband the Trek if they could arrive at a satisfactory settlement. Arthur Evans told James Kingsbury of the Toronto *Daily Star* that they were prepared to negotiate but that there would have to be a firm agreement rather than mere promises. "We want to see the agreement in black and white before we move out of here." [19] Evans also said that the Trek would not attempt to move east of Regina during negotiations but would proceed to Ottawa if no agreement could be reached.

June 17 turned out to be a very tense day for the trekkers, for the authorities, and probably for many Regina citizens as well. The strikers' publicity committee continued distributing their leaflets calling the public to be at the railway yards at 10 p.m. to see the trekkers off for Ottawa if the negotiations either collapsed or did not take place. "Only the mass support of Regina citizens will force the Authorities to keep their hands off us on our way to Ottawa." [20]

Assistant Commissioner Wood of the RCMP made elaborate preparations, coordinated with the CPR and its police, to prevent the boarding of trains. Wood mobilized all the forces at his command and also arranged with the CPR to cancel, unknown to the strikers, the eastbound freight expected to leave Regina at about 10 p.m. [21] Preparations were also made for reading the Riot Act if necessary.

The possibility of police actions provoking a riot further alarmed Premier Gardiner, who must have felt like a helpless bystander: he was unable to prevent the worsening of what appeared to be an explosive situation. Gardiner expressed his concern and annoyance during a meeting with T.C. Davis and J.W. Estey of the provincial cabinet and Manion and Weir on the morning of June 17. Manion described Gardiner's attitude in a report to the prime minister.

> Toward the end of his conversation he very emphatically said that if tonight, when the men were threatening to board the train at ten o'clock, there should be riots, so far as he and his Government were concerned they would order their police to deal with the rioters, who, they considered were not only those men who were threatening to board the train, but more emphatically the C.P.R. Police who were interfering with them, and he said that he would instruct his police to deal as severely with the C.P.R. Police as with the trekkers, because, he said, they were both equally guilty; in fact he considered the C.P.R. more guilty because they had permitted these men or even aided them to come thus far without interference.
>
> I expressed great surprise at his attitude, and said that he would be taking a very great responsibility, if he aided and abetted revolution in any such manner.[22]

There is no record of what specific orders, if any, were issued by Premier Gardiner to the police, nor is it clear to which police force he was referring. What Manion reported to Bennett may have been merely a spontaneous outburst by Gardiner, who was expressing what he would like to do. A telegram from the premier to the federal minister of Justice on the same day reiterated the Saskatchewan protest against federal intervention and declared that Ottawa would be responsible for any violence which might ensue.

> This constitutes taking the right to instruct the police in matters of administrative justice entirely out of our hands. In our opinion your action may result in causing a riot in this province endangering life and property. A letter just handed to the government by the police to the effect that preparations be made to read the Riot Act indicates you hold the same view. We protest your action as being unconstitutional and would state that your lack of action before these men left British Columbia to bring two forces to grips in Regina was bound to produce a riot in Saskatchewan if the present orders are carried out. We strongly protest this flouting of the constitutional rights of the province and would once more ask you to reconsider your position. Your appeal to us to cooperate in every way to protect lives and property as well as to maintain law and order has been made most difficult to comply with as you have taken unto yourself all the power consigned to the government under th B.N.A. Act to deal with such matters."[23]

Gardiner had obviously prepared his ground for any legal and political arguments which might follow a violent clash.

As it turned out, a violent confrontation was avoided on June 17 and a temporary compromise was worked out between the two federal ministers and representatives of the trekkers. Negotiations began at 2:15 p.m. in the Hotel Saskatchewan at a meeting between Manion and Weir and their assistants and eight representatives of the Trek, led by Arthur Evans. Evans, on the advice of Mayor Rink of Regina, had taken the initiative for getting the meeting underway by contacting Manion at his hotel that morning.[24] Also in attendance as observers—and indicating the widespread concern about the situation—were Mayor Rink and nine others representing the Canadian Legion, the Regina Ministerial Association, the Catholic Association, the Exhibition Board, the Public School Board, the Separate School Board, and the local Trades and Labour Council.

After an exchange of views and arguments concerning the grievances and demands of the relief camp strikers, the purpose of the camps, and the decision to stop the Trek, Manion proposed to the Trek representatives that they travel to Ottawa at government expense to put their grievances before the Bennett cabinet.[25] Meanwhile, the trekkers could either return to their homes or their camps or wait in Regina for their representatives to return. Manion emphasized that they had nothing to lose by accepting the proposal. The response of Evans and his delegation was that the proposal would have to be discussed by the rank and file before a decision could be made. A mass meeting of the trekkers would be held in the early evening and the Trek delegation would later call on the ministers to report the results.

There was considerable disagreement among both the leaders and the rank and file about the wisdom of accepting the government's offer. Some feared it might be a mere stalling tactic while the government prepared to smash the Trek or a trick to get the main leaders out of Regina. But to refuse the offer would make the trekkers appear unreasonable before public opinion. It was decided to accept the proposal provided that the government could guarantee certain conditions. A final agreement was worked out between Manion and Weir and the Trek leaders on the night of June 17. The agreement stipulated the following terms:[26]

(1) A deputation of eight were to journey to Ottawa at federal expense.

(2) The trekkers who remained in Regina were to be provided with three meal tickets per day at federal expense.

166

(3) The federal government was to pay for additional quarters and facilities for the trekkers in Regina.

(4) The federal authorities were to make no attempt to disrupt the Trek in the absence of their delegation to Ottawa.

(5) The delegation was to leave for Ottawa within thirty-six hours.

(6) The Trek leaders would not encourage additional unemployed to join their forces in Regina, but the 300 who were already expected to arrive from Dundurn would be accommodated.

(7) The trekkers would obey all laws and agree not to trespass on railway property in the absence of their delegation.

The temporary compromise reached at Regina seems to have been well received nationwide. It was generally applauded by both the Conservative and opposition press. The Montreal *Star,* which had condemned the Trek and supported the federal government, welcomed the compromise. "The news from Regina is the best that has come out of the West since the wild project of a mass descent of the unemployed upon Ottawa was launched."[27] Both sides were commended for their moderation.

> ...the encouraging thing is that an explosion in the Regina powder magazine has apparently been averted through a display of reasonableness on both sides. There has been no "gunplay"—not even a broken window.[28]

The Winnipeg *Free Press,* a Liberal newspaper which had been critical of the Bennett government, also welcomed the arrangement and supported the trekkers' demand for work and wages.

> The Government should be in sympathy with the request, for Mr. Bennett has referred at various times—he did so in one of his January broadcasts—to the necessity of providing for the unemployed in a satisfactory way which would maintain their morale.[29]

A violent clash appeared to have been averted. The Bennett government was now in a position to make some genuine concessions and achieve voluntary dispersal of the Trek. They would almost certainly have been congratulated by the press and opinion leaders and would have gained much needed political credibility in an election year. The RCWU and its supporters would have accepted any reasonable compromise and peacefully disbanded the Trek. They had already demonstrated during the big strike of December 1934 and on many lesser occasions both before and since that they were willing to be more than reasonable. They were not ultra-left adventurists nor did they harbour any illusions that a revolution was possible. A genuine compromise, however, would require some real concessions from the authorities. Vague promises of a rosier future were wearing thin after five years of unemployment.

Unfortunately, the federal government did not have the foresight to offer concessions designed to reach a genuine compromise. From the beginning they appear to have had no faith at all in negotiations. One of the main problems was that federal ministers, the DND and RCMP officials, the federal department of labour officials, and others who advised or made policy for the Bennett government, were working under false assumptions and prejudices about the nature of the RCWU leadership and the entire unemployed movement. They saw stereotypical wild-eyed "reds" who were unreasonable by nature. To them, any movement with communists in the leadership or which adopted radical or militant tactics was illegitimate by definition. It was partly this rigid attitude about "properly constituted authority" which had cost the Bennett government its credibility by 1935.

Federal ministers and other federal officials put little stock in negotiations from the time Manion and Weir visited Regina until the fateful meeting between the Trek delegation and the Bennett cabinet on June 22, and their reasoning revealed prejudice and inaccurate information about both the leaders and the composition of the Trek. In his original report to Bennett about the Regina meeting with the Trek representatives on the afternoon of June 17, Manion doubted that the government proposal for sending a delegation to Ottawa would be accepted

> as our best information is that their leaders are radicals of the most extreme type. [30]

Manion also wrote a lengthy memorandum to Bennett on June 20 in which he assumed—two days before the Trek leaders met the Bennett cabinet—that the negotiations in Ottawa would fail. [31] He foresaw clashes with authority in Regina and probably elsewhere which would require repressive measures.

> My conviction is that this Communistic crowd who are leading the more or less innocent unemployed are determined to stir up what would be practically a revolution and I feel that undoubtedly strong measures will have to be taken to curb this movement.

> Somehow the leaders should be got at and if possible got out of the position of leading these unemployed. [32]

Manion then made a number of suggestions as to how Bennett and the cabinet should handle the meeting with the trekkers' representatives. The suggestions were designed to improve the government's image but were based on the assumption that the Trek leaders did not want an agreement.

> ...my suggestions are made with the idea of getting the people generally behind us and away from that rather maudlin sympathy which they have toward these trekkers. The deputation, of course, does not want a satisfactory agreement and have, therefore, put up a number of proposals with that object in view. [33]

Manion then discussed the six trekkers' demands. He suggested that the first, regarding work and wages, was impossible, and that the government could make vague promises of minor concessions on the other five which dealt with workers' compensation, elected camp committees, control of the camps by the DND, unemployment insurance, and voting rights in federal elections.

> ...it seems to me that the others could in a general way, with some modifications, be accepted, not being too specific in the acceptance but showing the people generally that we are reasonable even to requests from a group like this. The future carrying out of the acceptance could be handled by yourself and modified in the best interests of the country as a whole. [34]

Manion also advised Bennett to emphasize what the government was already doing to relieve unemployment and to accede to a request from Mayor Ralph Webb of Winnipeg for a public works project to ease unemployment in that city. Bennett should also appeal to patriotism, which Manion described as "the importance of a reasonable Canadianism in a time like this when Canada is suffering part of a world condition." [35] Manion felt that such an approach by the prime minister would raise the morale of Conservative supporters and help swing public opinion behind the government in the event of confrontation with the trekkers.

> ...it will put a reasonable Canadian citizen in a mood to realize the situation and to support us if and when these trekkers come to a clash with the police at various parts of the country, as it seems to me they undoubtedly will do. [36]

Other federal officials, like Manion, based their planning and advice on the assumption that violent confrontations were virtually inevitable and a negotiated settlement out of the question. Assistant RCMP Commissioner Wood formulated an elaborate plan to forcibly suppress the Trek in Regina should the meetings of June 17 fail. He described his plan and his assessment of the situation in a memorandum to RCMP Commissioner MacBrien on June 18.[37] Wood felt certain that his plan, had there been an opportunity to implement it, would have put an end to the Trek. He based his assumption on a misconception concerning the type of people involved in the expedition.

> Energetic police action in this operation would, I am sure, have liquidated this movement, for a large percentage are boys who never have been in a relief camp and have joined this movement as they would a circus, not realizing what it was all about or what was back of it.[38]

Wood's description of the trekkers indicates either faulty RCMP intelligence reports or prejudiced interpretation of the evidence. He also expected that he would have to implement the plan soon.

> This plan will probably yet have to be put into effect, if the negotiations by the strikers' delegations fail, which I am inclined to believe will be the case.[39]

RCMP Commissioner MacBrien and officials of the federal department of labour in Regina and Ottawa, like Manion and Wood, based their assessments of the situation on the belief that the Ottawa negotiations would resolve nothing.[40] It would become a self-fulfilling prophecy.

Although the Trek leaders had originally been doubtful about the wisdom of going to Ottawa, they made the most of the new situation by rallying support for their cause on the journey eastward. The delegation was seen off by a large crowd of strikers and citizens who had gathered for a brief meeting in front of the Regina railway station in the early evening of June 18. Members of the delegation also addressed meetings en route to Ottawa during brief train stops at Brandon, Fort William, and Port Arthur.

The fact that the On-to-Ottawa trekkers had forced the federal government to begin any kind of negotiations spurred on the organized unemployed in other areas to put their grievances before the authorities. On their way back to Ottawa, Manion and Weir were met by a crowd of 500 unemployed at the Winnipeg station on June 18. Manion described the event in a report to Bennett.

> We were waited on at the Winnipeg station in passing through Tuesday night by five hundred unemployed who were very dictatorial in their demand that I should permit three of them to come East with the Regina group. This demand was turned down by myself on the ground that I had no right to deal with Winnipeg at all, but we had a pretty uncomfortable half or three-quarters of an hour interview with this unemployed group at Winnipeg.[41]

The organized unemployed were also on the move in Ontario and Quebec. A conference billed as the Ontario Hunger March Conference met in Toronto June 17-19 and appointed thirteen delegates who proceeded to Ottawa to demand an interview with the Bennett cabinet.[42] Some members of the delegation contacted the Regina representatives when they arrived in Ottawa. Delegates from the Val Cartier and Rockcliffe relief camps also contacted Evans and his group in Ottawa. They compared notes and attempted to coordinate their approach to the Bennett government. It seems that the unemployed protesters from Ontario and Quebec, where the relief camps were much quieter than in B.C., were looking to the leaders of the Trek for guidance in their own struggles.

The meeting between the On-to-Ottawa Trek delegation and the federal cabinet took place on Saturday morning, June 22.[43] Present were the eight strikers' representatives led by Arthur Evans and Prime Minister Bennett with eleven of his ministers and aides to take notes. The discussion became heated and degenerated into charges and counter charges which were later sensationalized by the press and left the trekkers and the federal government further apart than ever.

The meeting began calmly enough, with Evans, as spokesman for the delegation, presenting the main grievances of the camp workers. He presented his interpretation of the history of the RCWU and the struggle of the past several months and cited some specific grievances before going into the six demands of the Trek. Evans emphasized that individual grievances were not the major issue, but rather the nature of the relief camp system as a whole.

> We want to point out that the situation in British Columbia is not hot cakes and foremen. It is the absolute hopelessness of the relief camps for the Youth of Canada, and the question of hot cakes and foremen does not arise in the six demands of the charter

that has been developed and organized by the relief camp workers in the province of British Columbia.[44]

Evans concluded his initial remarks by complaining of a press report the previous day to the effect that sixty additional RCMP officers were being sent to Regina, charging that this was contrary to the agreement worked out with Manion and Weir whereby the federal government was not to disrupt the Trek during the absence of the delegation. At this point Manion interjected and insisted that the ministers had only agreed not to attempt to disrupt the Trek by propaganda. He in turn charged Evans with breaking the agreement by making public speeches en route to Ottawa.

At the conclusion of Evans' statement, the prime minister asked each of the delegates in turn where he was born. The fact that only Evans had been born in Canada was to be emphasized later by Bennett both in his remarks to the delegation and in his report to Parliament.

Bennett's interjection was followed by a brief statement by John Cosgrove of the delegation on workers' compensation and accidents in the work camps. The prime minister then proceeded to make his main statement. He began his remarks in anything but a conciliatory fashion by questioning the credibility of the trekkers' delegation on grounds which were of doubtful relevance to the issues at hand.

> We have listened with much interest as to what you men have had to say. With the exception of one of you, who has a record that we will not discuss, you were born outside Canada, and in the country from which you came I was told the other day there are one million men who have no work and never will have. In this country we have been passing through the same period of depression as the rest of the world.[45]

Bennett then proceeded with a brief exposition relating the fact that relief was a provincial matter but that in the case of the single unemployed the federal government had embarked upon the relief camp scheme because people were moving from province to province. He stated that there was no compulsion to go to the camps and claimed that the shelter, food and clothing were as good as that enjoyed by the average Canadian. Most of the single unemployed, said Bennett, were very appreciative of the camps.

It was after Bennett had described the relief camp system in a very positive light that he launched into a lengthy denunciation of communists, agitators, the Workers' Unity League, "Soviet Committees," "Communistic Boards" and the entire project of organizing the On-to-Ottawa Trek. He described the Trek as "a rising against law and against the institutions of our country" and claimed that the trekkers had gained public sympathy for a time but that people were beginning to realize "that you have been used [sic] better than most people in this country, provided with the facilities you had."[46]

> You have not shown much anxiety to get work, not much anxiety to get work. It is the one thing you do not want. What you want is this adventure in the hope that the organization which you are promoting in Canada may be able to over-awe government and break down the forces that represent law and order. I never thought that I would come to the day when I would hear a Canadian at any rate say that a country that sends its policemen west or east for the purpose of maintaining law in the country is going to be subjected to censure on the part of those who themselves admit they are violators of the law, admitted here today. The police have moved west; they have moved east; they will move in increasing numbers wherever it is necessary to maintain law. Take that down. Tell Mr. Cosgrove to take it down, Mr. Evans. Take that down. Make it clear that this government will not be over-awed by any such effort as that which has been made by those who in the name of sympathy have been able to impose upon the decent citizens of our country. Let me go one step further. You have raised the question of the food you have received. There are always abuses creeps into camps where some men, for instance, are lousy, and that is one of your complaints. Lice do not come from accidents. They are not of spontaneous production. They are taken into camp by somebody who is lousy and the lice spread. You know that, everyone knows that.[47]

The prime minister went on to assert that there was no justification for the trekkers' demands concerning workers' compensation and that the government had no intention of paying wages in the relief camps. There was then a brief exchange involving Bennett, Evans, and James Walsh from the delegation. It was at this point that Evans hurled his much quoted insult to the effect that Bennett was unfit to govern.

> You referred to us as not wanting to work. This is an insidious attempt to propagandize the press on your part, and anybody who professes to be Premier and uses such despicable tactics is not fit to be premier of a Hottentot village.[48]

173

Bennett responded by accusing Evans of being an embezzler for having been convicted of fraudulently converting union funds in 1924. Evans in turn called Bennett a liar and explained that he had illegally converted funds to assist striking miners and not for his own use. There followed an acrimonious exchange between Bennett and Evans and Cosgrove and O'Neil from the delegation during which the prime minister threatened to have Cosgrove removed from the room.

After this heated exchange, the prime minister completed his statement by explaining what his government had been doing about unemployment in general. He then dealt specifically with the trekkers' six demands. Paying wages in the camps was again pronounced impossible; workers' compensation was described as being mainly under provincial jurisdiction; the recognition of elected camp committees was denied and described as an attempt at "setting up Soviets." Bennett asserted that all individual complaints would be given a fair hearing. The demand that the relief camps be removed from the control of the DND was rejected. The demand for a system of social and non-contributing unemployment insurance was rejected, and on the matter of the right to vote it was asserted that the right already existed for all those who came within the provisions of the Franchise Act.

Bennett concluded his remarks by informing the delegation that the trekkers would be allowed to return to the camps and that they would be taken into consideration as work became available on highways and other public projects. They were again warned that illegal trespassing on the railways would not be tolerated.

Arthur Evans made the concluding remarks at the meeting. He indicated dissatisfaction at the cabinet response to the trekkers' demands and declared that, as far as he was concerned, the struggle against the government would continue.

> We are confronted today with a greater responsibility than when we first came here in view of the statement of the Prime Minister that the government will not deal with the questions raised here. In place of that they attempt to raise the red bogey and it appears that the Prime Minister has the red horrors of this government. Our responsibility is we must take this back to the workers and see that the hunger programme of Bennett is stopped.[49]

The meeting between the trekkers' delegation and the federal cabinet had obviously succeeded in increasing rather than decreasing antagonism between the two sides. And while it is clear both Prime

Minister Bennett and Arthur Evans indulged in intemperate and abusive remarks the minutes demonstrate that the main responsibility for the antagonistic atmosphere rested with Bennett.

Even before he began his main remarks the prime minister had insinuated that Evans was little better than a common criminal and attacked the legitimacy of the other seven delegates on the grounds that they were not born in Canada. Nothing was said about the fact that millions of Canadians, including many Members of Parliament and some of Bennett's own ministers, were not born in Canada. He then devoted a disproportionate part of his comments to denouncing communism and agitators and describing the Trek as merely a subversive conspiracy directed against constituted authority by men who did not want to work. The remarks about the men carrying lice into the camps could only be taken by the delegation as an additional insult. It was only after these statements that Evans resorted to denouncing Bennett as unfit to govern. And it was only after Bennett's attempt to misrepresent his criminal record that Evans declared the prime minister to be a liar.

A notable feature of the meeting was that there were no concessions whatsoever on any of the six demands. Bennett and his ministers had clearly disregarded the advice, offered by Manion in his memorandum of June 20, that they should appear conciliatory and make at least vaguely worded concessions.

While conceding nothing of either form or substance, Bennett made it clear that the Trek would be stopped, by force if necessary. After months of struggle, the Trek leaders had nothing of significance to take back to their supporters in Regina. They were left with no choice but to devise a means of continuing the Trek.

The next move of the trekkers' delegation was, in conjunction with representatives of the Ontario Hunger March and delegates from the Rockcliffe and Val Cartier relief camps, to call for a continuation and expansion of the Trek. The Ontario and Quebec delegations had interviewed the cabinet immediately following the Trek representatives and had met with a similar response. On the afternoon of June 22 the various delegations held a joint meeting to compare notes and plan the coordination of future activities. A joint statement was then issued under the names of Arthur Evans, Trek leader, Ernest Lawrie, President of the National Unemployed Council, and J. Bedard, representing the Ontario and Quebec delegates of the unemployed then in Ottawa. It stated that the Trek would continue, that within a few days a national call for the continuance and expansion of the expedition would be issued jointly by the executives of the Workers' Unity League, the Relief Camp Workers' Union, and the National Unemployed Council.

Arthur Evans and spokesmen for the other delegations addressed a public rally in the Rialto Theatre in Ottawa on Sunday, June 23. The meeting passed a resolution condemning the attitude of the Bennett cabinet towards representatives of the unemployed. That night the Trek delegation boarded a train for Regina. They had wired ahead to their supporters to organize railway station rallies at the various cities where the train would be stopping en route. The next phase of the struggle had begun.

Footnotes

1. Public Archives of Canada (PAC), *McNaughton Papers,* Vol. 61, File 380 (B), M.D. 12 to Defensor, June 14, 1935.
2. *Ibid.,* Vol. 60, File 380 (B), DOC 12 to Defensor, June 14, 1935 and June 15, 1935.
3. PAC, *Bennett Papers,* pp. 496599-600, Reports from Department of Labour Officials in Regina, June 15, 1935.
4. PAC, *Manion Papers,* Vol. 33, F.G. Bagshaw, E.C. Leslie, F. Somerville to Bennett, June 14, 1935.
5. James Kingsbury, Toronto *Daily Star,* June 15, 1935.
6. *Ibid.* The trekkers were given fairly widespread support from the CCF in Saskatchewan, though J.S. Woodsworth and the national party did not endorse the expedition and were critical of the RCWU leadership.
7. *Ibid.*
8. *Ibid.*
9. *Ibid.*
10. Regina *Leader-Post,* June 15, 1935.
11. Archives of Saskatchewan (A.S.), Regina Riot Inquiry Commission (RRIC). Proceedings, Exhibit 167, MacBrien to Wood, June 13, 1935.
12. RRIC Proceedings, Exhibit 177, MacBrien to Wood, June 15, 1935.
13. "Railways Give Formal Word Halt Riders," Regina *Daily Star,* June 15, 1935.
14. *McNaughton Papers, op. cit.,* McNaughton memorandum on telephone conversation with Boak, June 17, 1935.
15. PAC, *W.L.M. King Papers,* File 2119, Gardiner to Bennett, June 15, 1935.
16. *Ibid.,* File 2119, Guthrie to Gardiner, June 15, 1935.
17. William Marchington, "Two Ministers Leave Ottawa for Saskatchewan Capital," Toronto *Globe,* June 15, 1935.
18. Ottawa *Journal,* June 17, 1935.

19. James Kingsbury, "Ottawa Trek Halts to Await Ministers," Toronto *Daily Star*, June 15, 1935.
20. *Manion Papers, op. cit.,* Vol. 33, "On-to-Ottawa," leaflet prepared by the publicity committee of the relief camp strikers.
21. *McNaughton Papers, op. cit.,* memorandum of telephone conversation between McNaughton and Boak, June 17, 1935.
22. *Manion Papers, op. cit.,* Vol. 33, Manion memorandum to Bennett, June 17, 1935.
23. RRIC Exhibits, Gardiner to Guthrie, June 17, 1935. Also cited in Victor Hoar (ed.), *Recollections of the On-to-Ottawa Trek* by Ronald Liversedge (McClelland and Stewart Ltd., 1973), p. 183.
24. *Manion Papers, op. cit.,* Vol. 33, minutes of meeting between ministers and Trek representatives, June 17, 1935.
25. *Ibid.*
26. *Ibid.,* Vol. 33, night letter of Manion to Bennett, June 17, 1935.
27. Montreal *Star*, June 18, 1935. Clipping in *Manion Papers, op. cit.,* Vol. 33.
28. *Ibid.*
29. Winnipeg *Free Press*, June 20, 1935.
30. *Manion Papers, op. cit.,* Vol. 33, Manion to Bennett, afternoon of June 17. Also reprinted in Hoar, *op. cit.,* p. 187.
31. *Bennett Papers, op. cit.,* pp. 496622-24, Manion to Bennett, June 20, 1935.
32. *Ibid.*
33. *Ibid.*
34. *Ibid.*
35. *Ibid.*
36. *Ibid.*
37. RRIC Exhibits, memorandum from Wood to MacBrien, June 18, 1935. Also reprinted in Hoar, *op. cit.,* pp. 187-90.
38. *Ibid.*
39. *Ibid.*
40. RRIC Exhibits, MacBrien to Wood, June 19, 1935 and Burgess to Hereford, June 19, 1935. Also cited in Gladys Stone, "The Regina Riot," unpublished M.A. thesis, University of Saskatchewan, 1967, p. 65.
41. Bennett Papers, *op. cit.,* pp. 476622-24, Manion to Bennett, June 20, 1935.
42. *Ibid.,* p. 496631, W.G. Harris (secretary for delegation of Ontario Hunger March Conference) to Bennett, June 21, 1935.
43. *RRIC Report,* "Interview of Trek Delegation with Cabinet," June 22, 1935. Also reprinted in Hoar, *op. cit.,* pp. 194-220. This is a verbatim report of the meeting in the form of minutes, including everything which was said by everyone from the delegation and the cabinet. All quotations and references here will be based on these minutes.
44. *Ibid.*

45. *Ibid.* When Bennett referred to "the country from which you came" he apparently meant Britain but he was not entirely correct in his information. Of the seven Trek delegates not born in Canada four came from Britain and the others from Ireland, Newfoundland, and Denmark.
46. *Ibid.*
47. *Ibid.*
48. *Ibid.*
49. *Ibid.*

CHAPTER X
The Regina Riot

On June 22, 1935, federal DND and RCMP officials began putting into action their plans for stopping the Trek in Regina and preventing resumption of the expedition from some other point such as Calgary, Edmonton, or Winnipeg. Winnipeg was considered a particularly troublesome area: the RCMP had reported to the local District Officer Commanding (DOC) that 860 men had already registered to join the Trek and the number might reach 1000 when the expedition reached town.[1]

On June 24 Brigadier Boak, DOC in Regina, was instructed to establish a special camp near Lumsden, about twenty miles from Regina. The plan was that, after the federal government commitment to feed the strikers expired on Wednesday, June 26, when the Trek delegation returned to Regina, the trekkers would be forced into the special camp pending their dispersal to the regular camps. Assistant Commissioner Wood of the RCMP had recommended this move.

> Absolutely essential that housing and particularly feeding be handed over to National Defence Department in order to secure control and liquidate movement.[2]

The Lumsden camp would be nominally under the department of labour for political reasons but would be administered by military officers and policed by the RCMP.[3] While the DND would be in charge of the camp and the RCMP of the policing, the official director and man in charge of public relations for the operation would be C.P. Burgess, senior representative of the federal department of labour in Regina.[4]

The federal government also mounted a coordinated public relations campaign to discredit the Trek leaders. It began when Bennett announced to the House of Commons the establishment of the special camp accompanied by a federal offer to provide transportation for those trekkers wishing to return to their original camps or their homes. Bennett also gave his version of the meeting with the Trek delegation two days before, managing to discredit the men in a few short sentences. "The spokesman was one Arthur H. Evans. The other seven admitted they were not born in Canada. Evans was the only Canadian born of the eight. He himself has a criminal record."[5] The Trek leaders were also portrayed as determined to destroy law and order by "taking men who were in experienced and young and exploiting them for the purposes of advancing their sinister purposes."[6] The prime minister's statement ended with the warning that the federal government fully intended to stop the Trek, which was "in reality an organized effort on the part of the various communist organizations throughout Canada to effect the overthrow of constituted authority in defiance of the laws of the land."[7]

The idea of the trekkers as innocents being misled by ruthless "reds" was emphasized repeatedly by federal officials in the last days of June. To the government it may have seemed like good propaganda, but it also appears that some officials believed in this explanation themselves. Thus Assistant Commissioner Wood in a report to RCMP headquarters on June 25 claimed to have modified the attitude of local opinion leaders towards the federal government's position by acquainting them with the criminal record and communist connections of the Trek leaders.[8] Wood also hoped to change the minds of some of the trekkers by the same methods.

> There are no apparent signs of defection in the strikers' camp at the present time, although I understand there are a considerable number of men who object to being classed as 'Reds' and are only now learning the true nature of the leaders and their connection with the Communist Party.[9]

These tactics were employed when the federal department of labour issued an official notice to the strikers on June 25 informing them that after the morning of June 26 there would be no meal tickets provided in Regina and the men could obtain food and accommodation in the special camp near Lumsden pending arrangements for their return to their homes or the regular camps. The notice contained a section designed to turn the rank and file trekkers against their leadership.

180

> The Dominion Government recognizes that many of those now congregated at Regina on the 'On-to-Ottawa' trek are young men who have been misled by their leaders, the majority of whom are acting and taking their directions from the Communist Bureau of Canada, with a view to upsetting constituted authority. There is, therefore, no doubt that many desire to return either to their homes, where such exist or to the Relief Camps...[10]

It is highly unlikely that this type of appeal enhanced the cause of the federal government. It may even have had a negative effect. Aside from the fact that it was an official notice from the Bennett government, which was distrusted and disliked by the trekkers, it was very patronizing in tone and assumed that the trekkers were political illiterates. Arthur Evans had been organizing among the camp workers since 1934 and had been recognized as the main leader of the strikers since the walkout from the B.C. camps in early April. He was popular among the trekkers and had never made a secret of the fact that he was a communist.

By the time they issued their notice of June 25 federal officials had made all the arrangements for disbanding the Trek, by the use of armed force if necessary. The special camp near Lumsden had been constructed. The RCMP had been reinforced and Assistant Commissioner Wood had made special arrangements with the Regina city police and the railway police. Available RCMP personnel would number about 340 and with railway and city police the numbers would be close to 500. Wood therefore estimated that he could deal with the situation without calling in the military.[11] Although Wood was receiving cooperation from the Regina city police he was unsure of what to expect from City Council as they had not been cooperative in the recent past.

> I am not sure of the attitude of the City Council as a statement addressed to the public through the press, asking the public to keep away from the railway yards on the night of the 17th when trouble was anticipated and to support law and order, was refused signature by the Mayor and consequently not made public.[12]

Wood also reported to the RCMP commissioner that he would not approach the mayor for further support until he considered the time ripe.

> Referring to your suggestion that the Mayor be requested to prohibit further parades, this action will be taken in due course,

when the situation has developed to the stage where the strikers have forfeited public support. [13]

From his report to RCMP Commissioner MacBrien of June 25, it appears that Wood expected public support for the Trek to decline after a violent clash between the trekkers and the police. The last meal ticket provided by the federal government for the trekkers was for breakfast on June 26. From 8 a.m. that day C.P. Burgess would be operating an office in the Grain Show Building at the Regina Exhibition Grounds to receive registrations for the special Lumsden camp. Wood's comments indicate that he did not expect many registrations for the camp or voluntary dispersal of the Trek until after a violent confrontation between the trekkers and the police. He also implied that such a clash might be precipitated by the police because the trekkers did not want to risk losing public support.

> It is not expected that there will be many voluntary registrations tomorrow and that sooner or later there will be a demonstration in front of Mr. Burgess' office which will bring about Police action. The situation is suitable for our purposes in that it is opposite the Armouries and there is a large open space in all directions surrounding the building where we could use mounted men to advantage. Following any such clash between the police and the strikers, I anticipate there will be a movement then toward voluntary registration and dispersion. This arrangement will, in all probability relieve the City of any disturbance in their main streets as I have in mind that the strikers will endeavour to keep the public support and sympathy as long as possible. The slogan among them is that Regina citizens will see them out of Regina... [14]

Wood stated in the same report that he did not think that the trekkers would even resort to nuisance parades or occupying restaurants or stores because of the importance of maintaining public support.

At that time the assistant commissioner's plan for dispersing the Trek, whether or not a violent clash developed, involved two options. One would have the police surrounding the trekkers within their sleeping quarters in Exhibition Stadium and allowing them outside only in small groups for the purposes of registering for the special Lumsden camp. The other option was for the police to occupy the premises and take possession of the trekkers' packsacks when they were absent at a mass meeting. In the first case they could presumably be starved into submission, and in the second they could be forced to negotiate for the return of their personal belongings and a place to sleep.

While federal officials were preparing for a showdown, Premier Gardiner as well as the trekkers and their local supporters were attempting to devise a means whereby the Trek could proceed beyond Regina. On June 24 a delegation of trekkers and supporters interviewed the premier. They wanted to determine the general attitude of the provincial government to the continuation of the Trek and whether the province could force the railways to move the men out of Saskatchewan or would provide them with alternative transportation. [16] Gardiner received the delegation sympathetically but was vague in his replies and made no commitment. He expressed the opinion that the railways had assisted the strikers in getting to Saskatchewan and should carry them through. The premier also stated that, since the federal authorities were instructing the RCMP, the province was in no position to take action. [17]

When they returned to Regina on June 26 the Trek leaders interviewed Gardiner and requested that the provincial government secure the trekkers against police interference while in the province, provide relief until they could leave Saskatchewan, and provide financial assistance for transportation to Winnipeg. Gardiner replied that to obtain relief the trekkers would have to apply to the city as ordinary transients, that the federal authorities had assumed control of the RCMP, and that he was not going to create a problem for Manitoba as others had done for Saskatchewan. It was clear that Gardiner would do nothing to encourage the trekkers to stay in Saskatchewan, yet he would not provide them with financial assistance to get to Manitoba. He did not want to let the federal government "off the hook" and be held responsible for what might happen later in another province.

The trekkers attempted to obtain relief from the city but met with no success and, therefore, were left with the alternative of depending upon their own dwindling resources or going to Lumsden, which they refused to do. Gardiner feared that the denial of relief except at Lumsden might force the trekkers into drastic action which would lead to a violent confrontation with the police. On June 26 he sent two telegrams to Bennett. [18] The first protested the establishment of the Lumsden camp and again insisted that the trekkers be allowed to leave Saskatchewan. The second offered to feed the men for at least one more day at provincial expense to decrease the chance of violence. The prime minister declined the offer on the grounds that food and shelter were available at Lumsden. The federal strategy was to force the strikers into the Lumsden camp by hunger if necessary.

By now polemical telegrams were being exchanged daily between the two levels of government over who had the power to enforce law in Saskatchewan. When Bennett chastised Gardiner for allegedly failing to maintain law and order, Gardiner charged that the federal authorities had usurped the power guaranteed to the provinces by the constitution.

> Throughout the whole course of this matter your Government has acted without our knowledge, consent or concurrence and took complete charge of our police force and assumed the unquestionable functions of a provincial government. You and you alone have prevented this Government from fulfilling our constitutional responsibilities. If you desire to publicly withdraw from that position and place us where we can assume our constitutional obligations kindly wire us accordingly. [19]

Bennett bluntly refused to so so and accused Gardiner of refusing to defend the existing social order against communist designs.

> Have not the slightest intention of withdrawing from the position which we have taken and proposed to use our utmost endeavour even though you decline to cooperate to maintain the fabric of our society and the institutions of the country against the illegal threats and demands of communists and their associates. [20]

The federal government soon moved into other areas of provincial jurisdiction. The RCMP were given orders not only to prevent trespassing on the railways but also to prevent strikers leaving Regina by truck, car, bus, or on foot. [21] This made the legal situation more complex, as highway travel was under the jurisdiction of the provincial department of highways.

On June 26 a mass meeting of trekkers endorsed a plan to move east by highway. An appeal was made to local supporters for trucks, however a sufficient number of trucks could not be obtained, because, it seems, warnings had been issued to trucking firms by the RCMP. [22] The trekkers, with cooperation from the provincial government and financial support from local businessmen, decided to make a test case of the legalities of the situation. [23] They arranged for one truck and two private cars to leave the city on the evening of June 27. The office of the provincial Highway Commission remained open late that afternoon and a permit was issued allowing a truck owner to carry passengers to the Manitoba boundary. That afternoon Assistant

184

Commissioner Wood announced publicly that he had been instructed to prevent all trekkers from leaving the city by whatever means. The truck and two cars were intercepted outside of Regina in the early evening and six drivers and passengers, including Reverend Sam East of Regina, were arrested. The vehicles were impounded.

Assistant Commissioner Wood was not certain of his legal authority for making the arrests and it appears that RCMP Commissioner MacBrien was not entirely certain either. MacBrien initially informed Wood that the federal government was taking action under the "peace, order and good government" clause of the Relief Act which would provide the RCMP with the legal authority to make the arrests.

> ...confirming my telephone conversation with you, Government is taking action under Relief Measures Act declaring national emergency so as to maintain peace, order and good government. This will protect you against such action and seizures which you consider it necessary to take with regard to present situation affecting camp strikers in Regina. [24]

As it turned out, on the morning of June 28, the federal department of justice instructed F.B. Bagshaw and E.C. Leslie, Regina barristers, to charge the arrested men under Section 98 of the Criminal Code. Bagshaw informed the RCMP that, pending receipt of further information regarding Section 98, they should charge five of the men, Reverend East having been released, with vagrancy. [25]

The federal government "action" referred to in MacBrien's instructions to Wood was what was later referred to as the "phantom" order-in-council which was allegedly passed under the section of the Relief Act which stated that "the Governor in Council may, when Parliament is not in session, take all such measures as in his discretion may be deemed advisable to maintain, within the competence of Parliament, peace, order and good government throughout Canada..." It was reported in the press that those trekkers arrested leaving Regina on the evening of June 27 had been charged under the authority of such an order-in-council. [26] Wood also issued a public statement carried in Regina newspapers on June 28 to the effect that anyone who assisted the trekkers with food, shelter, accommodation or transportation would be liable to prosecution under the order-in-council. [27]

In fact, no such order-in-council had been passed, though Wood may have believed for a short time that it had been. The cabinet had no legal authority to pass such an order-in-council under the

Relief Act because Parliament was then sitting. On the day that Wood made his statement (June 28) Attorney-General Davis wired Justice Minister Hugh Guthrie inquiring under what authority the Ottawa government had acted in ordering the arrests of the previous night. Guthrie replied that the RCMP had been instructed to arrest the trekkers for any breaches of the law which might include vagrancy, unlawful travel on the highways, or Section 98.[28] On June 29, in response to a further inquiry from Davis, Guthrie replied that no order-in-council of any kind had been passed in connection with the Regina situation. The federal authorities had obviously taken it upon themselves to instruct the RCMP in Saskatchewan in the enforcement of the ordinary criminal law and not merely in matters coming under the Railway Act. This represented a violation of provincial jurisdiction. RCMP officials had also stated publicly that they were acting under legal authority granted by an order-in-council which did not exist.

The statements by Wood carried in the Regina newspapers had the desired effect. On June 29 the Citizens' Emergency Committee reported that they were unable to obtain sufficient food and supplies from the public for the further sustenance of the trekkers.[29] Citizens were fearful of defying what they assumed to be a legal prohibition. The RCMP order forbidding assistance also created tension within the Citizens' Emergency Committee over whether it was advisable to defy legal authority. Most of the Trades and Labour Council members withdrew from the committee.[30]

By June 28 the federal government had also decided to arrest the leaders of the Trek under Section 98 of the Criminal Code. It was decided that the RCWU would be declared an unlawful association and therefore that anyone belonging to it would be subject to prosecution under Section 98. The report of the Regina Riot Inquiry Commission (RRIC) describes the instructions which were issued to Assistant Commissioner Wood on June 28.

> On the morning of the 28 Colonel Wood was advised by the Commissioner by telephone that the Government desired the arrest of the leaders as soon as possible. During the conversation Colonel Wood stated that so far as he knew the leaders had done nothing in the province to warrant their arrest. On the same day, however, the Commissioner instructed him by telegram that the Government desired proceedings taken under Section 98 of the Criminal Code against those arrested on the evening of the 27 and also against the known leaders, Evans, Black, O'Neil, Shaw and "others you think are necessary." He was also advised that a special agent, Leopold, who had experience in Communist

activities, would arrive in Regina on Monday morning, July 1st, with documents for perusal by counsel. At his request information in possession of the officers commanding at Vancouver and Edmonton was forwarded to Colonel Wood and on the morning of July 1st was placed before counsel for consideration.[31]

It was announced publicly that the federal government was invoking Section 98 and this was carried as a major news story across the country. RCMP headquarters in Ottawa placed the broadest possible interpretation on the potentialities of Section 98 and these were elaborated upon and emphasized in news reports. One such report, under the heading "Will Class All In Strike Body as Communists," appeared in the Toronto *Daily Star*.

> All strikers holding membership in any of the strike organizations are to be considered communists, it was officially stated at R.C.M.P. headquarters today. Under this ruling, Section 98 of the Criminal Code is being invoked and any striker trying to trek from one province to another is considered a Communist and liable to arrest as such. Any person giving aid or comfort to any such person is also liable to prosecution. R.C.M.P. senior officers said this included the relief camp workers' associations and similar bodies which are affiliated with the Workers' Unity League. The leaders are declared to be known Communists.[32]

The actual orders to the RCMP in Regina were to arrest only the leaders and there were no plans to arrest hundreds of people, but it is easy to see how an impression would be created. It was already public knowledge that the people arrested east of Regina on June 27 were being charged under Section 98, and they had, in fact, been "trying to trek from one province to another."

Adding to public apprehension was the fact that federal officials made no attempt to reassure the public that the so-called "phantom" order-in-council had not been passed. Guthrie had so informed Attorney-General Davis but there was no public announcement to this effect. Newspapers carried reports on June 28 and June 29 based on the assumption that such an order-in-council existed.

In response to inquiries from reporters federal officials did not deny its existence; they merely refused to discuss the question. This allowed reporters to speculate about the contents of the non-existent order-in-council and some did so with abandon. The Toronto *Daily Star* carried an article under the banner headline "See 'Magna Carta' Scrapped by Bennett" in which canada was described as "in the unique position of operating a criminal law which the government

187

refuses to make public."[33] The reporter assumed the existence of the order-in-council, based on Wood's public statement of June 28, but had been unable to obtain information about it.

> At the Prime Minister's Office and the office of the privy council, there was a flat refusal today to discuss the terms of an order-in-council passed Wednesday under the "peace, order and good government" clause of the Relief Act...[34]

Another article in the same issue of the *Daily Star* was based on the same assumptions and referred to similar difficulties.

> R.C.M.P. headquarters were silent about the secret order-in-council passed by the government on Wednesday, giving them further power. Attempts to obtain copies of the order-in-council met with refusal at the privy council office and the Department of Justice professed ignorance of any such order.[35]

Grant Dexter wrote an article which was carried in the Regina *Leader-Post* of June 29 about the federal government's involvement in secret activities.

> The Bennett government Friday executed a dramatic and mysterious move vitally affecting the status of the trekking battalions of unemployed men now concentrated at Regina.
> Despite the utmost that Ottawa correspondents could do the nature of the move remained undisclosed. Mr. Bennett, it appears, is the author and he alone was cited as the source of information. He held his own counsel.
> From the West came queries to Ottawa declaring that whatever action had been taken the net result was to prevent camp strikers from using roads, to prohibit citizens from providing them with food, lodging or transportation.[36]

Local supporters of the trekkers in Regina could perhaps be forgiven if they felt intimidated. It was known that men had been arrested and charged under Section 98; the RCMP had issued orders forbidding assistance to the trekkers; and there was widespread speculation about an order-in-council and other measures which the federal authorities had undertaken or were about to undertake.

The trekkers' own resources were exhausted. There was no financial help from any level of government and the public had been forbidden to assist them. And they refused to place themselves in the hands of the DND at Lumsden. It was decided to discontinue the Trek and attempt to make arrangements with provincial or federal authorities for an orderly retreat. The idea was that the trekkers would, with government assistance, return under their own organization to British Columbia and other localities where men had joined the expedition.

While the Trek leaders were devising a strategy for an orderly retreat, Assistant Commissioner Wood was under pressure from RCMP headquarters in Ottawa to proceed with arrests under Section 98. Commissioner MacBrien called Wood on the morning of June 30 to ask him if he had carried out the arrests of the leaders.[37] Wood believed that there was still insufficient evidence to justify the arrests. Documents from Vancouver and Edmonton would not arrive until the next day, July 1, and Wood thought that counsel would be several days examining them before reaching a decision.[38]

On July 1 the Trek leaders initiated negotiations with both federal and provincial officials in the hope of obtaining an agreement for an early withdrawal. Arthur Evans contacted C.P. Burgess, the chief federal representative in Regina, and requested a meeting of federal, provincial and Trek representatives. Burgess refused to meet with provincial officials but agreed to a meeting with Trek representatives at 10:30 a.m.[39] Present at the meeting were Evans and several of his associates and Burgess and his aides, including an RCMP stenographer.

Evans stated that the trekkers were prepared to return to the camps and localities from which they had come under their own organization and jurisdiction. They requested relief and medical supplies while arrangements for departure were being made and it was expected this would take two or three days. The delegation also requested immunity from prosecution for everyone except Evans for any previous activities associated with the Trek.

Burgess suggested the trekkers go to the Lumsden camp, but this was not acceptable to the delegation. Evans' remarks indicated that the Trek leaders desired to end the stalemate peacefully without the appearance of total capitulation on the part of the strikers. The RRIC report, which was generally extremely critical of the RCWU, portrayed Evans attitude and proposals as eminently reasonable.

> In making these proposals Evans' stated that they should not be regarded as a capitulation on the part of the strikers because he thought that results would follow from what had already been accomplished and he also said he had no desire to engage the strikers in a blood bath and that they "conscientiously" desired to open negotiations with the Federal Government.[40]

Burgess informed the Trek delegation that he would have to contact Ottawa before making any definite commitments and agreed to meet them again at 2:30 p.m.

At this stage federal officials in Ottawa refused to take advantage of what was probably an excellent opportunity to reach a peaceful compromise. In fact, Assistant Commissioner Wood and Commissioner MacBrien of the RCMP had suggested that they might attempt negotiations for the disbandment of the Trek from Exhibition Stadium though they did not make it clear whether they were suggesting that the trekkers be allowed to disband under their own organization. The Ottawa authorities refused any compromise whatsoever and Burgess was instructed by the federal Commissioner of Unemployment Relief that the men *must* disband from either Lumsden or Dundurn.[41] Federal officials in Regina were prevented from engaging in any serious negotiations at all, and this ruled out a possible compromise on some variation of the trekkers' request that they disband under their own organization.

Burgess, accompanied by Wood and Inspector Walter Mortimer of the RCMP, met the Trek delegation at 2:30 p.m. and informed them that they would have to disband under federal auspices at either Dundurn or Lumsden. The Trek delegation could not accept this, and, there being nothing to negotiate, the meeting adjourned.

The Regina Riot Inquiry Commission considered the disagreement over how to disperse the Trek to be the crucial factor leading to the breakdown in negotiations. "The rock upon which the delegation and the officials of the Dominion Government split was the place and method of disbandment." The Inquiry Commissioners also believed that if federal officials had been allowed some flexibility by Ottawa a compromise agreement might have been achieved.[43]

The Trek leaders, having failed to move the federal officials, met with Premier Gardiner at 5 p.m. The delegates made the same proposals to Gardiner as they had made to Burgess earlier in the day, but they also offered to be dispersed under provincial government auspices if they were not allowed to disband under their own organization.[44] Gardiner told the delegation that their proposals would be considered and they would be informed of the government's decision late that night or early the next morning. The premier then arranged for a meeting at 8 that evening of those members of his cabinet who were in Regina—many being out of town for the July 1 holiday.

Assistant Commissioner Wood and his associates were preparing for the arrest of the strike leaders at about the same time that the delegation was conferring with Premier Gardiner. When Wood returned to his office from the afternoon meeting with the Trek delegates he discovered that the counsel retained by the federal government was prepared to issue warrants for the arrest of Evans and six other leaders of the Trek under Section 98.[45] E.C. Leslie, F.B. Bagshaw, and Sergeant Leopold of the Security and Intelligence Branch of the RCMP, who had arrived that morning from Ottawa, had been examining documents forwarded from the RCMP in Edmonton and Vancouver.[46] They claimed that there was sufficient evidence to declare the RCWU an unlawful association.

Wood conferred with several of his officers and decided to make the arrests within the next few hours. The haste in carrying out the arrests seems surprising in view of the fact that Wood had expected counsel to take several days to examine the evidence before reaching a decision. The assistant commissioner explained some of the reasoning behind the decision in his testimony before the Regina Riot Inquiry Commission.

> I recognized in these warrants the leaders of the strikers and members of the strategy committee. It was recognized by our police heads that the arrest of those leaders, and particularly the members of the strategy committee, which were the brains of their organization, would facilitate greatly the negotiations with the body of the strikers to induce them to return home and disband.[47]

Neither Assistant Commissioner Wood nor anyone else informed the provincial authorities that the RCMP were about to arrest the Trek leaders.[48] The arrests and the resulting rioting took provincial officials completely by surprise. Attorney-General Davis, who left the city to spend a few days at a nearby resort on June 29, had been informed by Wood before he left that no immediate action was contemplated. Davis had arranged for the Deputy Attorney-General to contact Wood by telephone periodically and inform him of any new developments. The deputy contacted Wood on the morning of July 1 and then telephoned Davis to pass on the word that no action was expected. The explanations offered later by Wood for his failure to inform the provincial authorities of the change of plans that afternoon and the impending arrests were that he believed both Davis and Gardiner to be out of town and, in any event, he was fully occupied preparing for the arrests.[49]

The failure to inform provincial authorities was even more amazing in view of the fact that C.P. Burgess knew that the Trek leaders were meeting provincial officials in the late afternoon or evening of July 1.[50] Evidence indicates that Wood and other RCMP officials probably also knew though they denied it later in testimony before the Inquiry Commission.[51]

Having decided to make the arrests, Wood and his associates proceeded with arrangements almost immediately. It was the nature of those arrangements and the means by which they were carried out which provoked what has been referred to ever since as the Regina Riot.

Wood and his officers, according to their testimony before the Regina Riot Inquiry Commission, had discussed various possibilities for effecting the arrests of the Trek leaders.[52] Exhibition Stadium was rejected on the grounds that there would be large numbers of strikers in the vicinity. Arresting the leaders on the streets was ruled out on the grounds that it would be difficult to arrest them all at once and simultaneous arrests were considered important "in order to remove at one stroke the effective leadership of the trek."[53]

The plan finally decided upon was to arrest the leaders at Unity Centre, the headquarters of the Trek, or at the beginning of a mass meeting in the evening on Market Square. The meeting, which would attract a crowd of between 1500 and 2000, had been called to inform Regina supporters of the latest developments concerning the Trek. It was designed for citizens rather than trekkers, most of whom would be attending a ball game at the exhibition grounds.

No explanation was ever offered as to why Wood and his officers did not decide to wait until the meeting was over and then arrest the leaders after the crowd had left. The logistics would surely have been no more complicated than the elaborate arrangements which were made for executing the arrests at the beginning of the meeting.

The plan was that the arrests would be made by plain-clothesmen stationed around the platform and throughout the crowd. They would attempt to make the seven arrests simultaneously and remove the arrested men to a nearby police van. Supposedly to prevent the possibility of escape and to protect the plain clothesmen, policemen surrounded the square on all sides. Three troops of RCMP surrounded the square on three sides, concealed in furniture vans. A troop of city police was inside the garage of the Regina Police Station which bordered the square on the east side. A troop of mounted RCMP were stationed two blocks from market square.

These were elaborate arrangements for the arrest of seven people and raise serious questions about why Wood chose to arrest the leaders in front of a mass meeting of their supporters. One would have thought that a police officer of Wood's experience could have devised a more discreet and less provocative arrangement and still carried off the arrests successfully. Obviously he was intent upon not only arresting the leaders but also making a show of force of the type he described in the telegram to RCMP Commissioner MacBrien on June 24. With the leaders arrested and the police having demonstrated that they could firmly control the situation, the trekkers would have no alternative but to disband under the conditions laid down by the federal government.

The plan described by Wood was that the plain-clothesmen would make the arrests at a signal from a police whistle. The RCMP and city police were then to move out of the vans and the garage but supposedly not to advance upon the crowd unless resistance was offered, the arresting officers were endangered, or the leaders were about to escape. Chief Bruton of the city police testified that he understood the police were to advance upon the crowd as soon as the whistle sounded. [54]

What happened at the fateful moment was that two troops of RCMP descended from their vans a moment before the whistle sounded, their officers claiming later that they thought they had heard the signal. The whistle then sounded and not only did the plain-clothesmen move to make the arrests but the doors of the police garage were flung open and the city police advanced rapidly upon the crowd. The RRIC report described them as advancing "at the double in close formation towards the platform."[55] They were armed with children's baseball bats which the police department had on hand for occasions of this nature. [56]

Gladys Stone describes this incident with a quotation from the Regina *Daily Star.*

> A whistle blew. The four doors of the city garage at the rear of the headquarters building, not 100 feet from the speakers stand, swung upward with a clatter and blue uniformed, helmeted constables, as well as plainclothes officers, ran out waving "baseball bat" batons overhead. People began to run. [57]

At the same time, the RCMP troops advanced upon the square and were quickly engaged in hand to hand combat with members of the crowd. [58]

Witnesses before the Inquiry Commission described the dispersal of the crowd by the police.

> A great deal of evidence was given as to the methods used by the City Police in dispersing the crowd. One witness described

it as "swinging their batons and knocking down any persons they could get hold of," another says, "They struck wherever the batons wanted to fall." Another says, "I saw them hitting people with their clubs." At least ten witnesses have given evidence upon this subject and the above quotations are indications of the general trend of their testimony with respect to it. [59]

There seems to be no doubt that the police provoked the riot. In modern parlance it would be described as a "police riot." Even the RRIC report, which was generally biased in favour of the police, conceded that police action was a factor in setting off the rioting.

...the presence of the three troops of police in the vicinity, one of which was advancing towards the crowd, necessarily created some alarm among the people gathered on the Square and lent colour to the belief, which no doubt some of them entertained, that the police had come upon the Square for the purpose of breaking up a peaceable and orderly meeting. [60]

The police quickly cleared the square and the large crowd of Regina citizens and trekkers scattered into the surrounding streets. Most of the Regina residents attempted to make for the safety of their homes. The 200-300 trekkers attempted to form into groups and march to their headquarters at Exhibition Stadium. Word was also sent to the exhibition grounds that the meeting had been broken up but the main body of trekkers should secure the stadium and stay there. [61] On no account were they to attempt to come downtown where they could be attacked and scattered by squads of mounted and foot police. Some had already left for the city centre upon hearing of the fighting but the majority remained at the stadium.

To ward off attacks by squads of mounted police the trekkers overturned cars and used them as barricades. Rocks and other missiles could then be thrown from behind the barricades at lines of charging horsemen. On other streets the tactic was for strikers armed with rocks to form two or three lines. The first line would throw rocks at advancing horse or foot police and then fall to their knees for the second line to get their rocks away. It was during one of these battles that a squad of foot police first drew their revolvers and fired into the trekkers—wounding several trekkers and bystanders. There was additional shooting by police in the course of the evening. There was no shooting by trekkers or their supporters—none of whom were carrying firearms.

There was a great deal of evidence, including many eyewitness accounts, presented to the Regina Riot Inquiry Commission (RRIC) to the effect that there were several instances where individual policemen or small groups of policemen "ran amok" and brutally attacked both trekkers and innocent bystanders. Some attacks seemed to be totally without provocation. The Inquiry Commission related much of this evidence but argued that it could not be true on the grounds that they could not believe policemen would commit such actions.

> Such, for instance, is the case of three mounties pounding a man on the ground; three mounties and a city policeman beating one striker, one policeman clubbing an unconscious man near the General Theatre; four city policemen beating one striker; city police marching west on 11th AVenue shooting as they went, assault of one Belabek on July 2nd by Sergeant Logan.[62]

The Commission dismissed these eyewitness accounts by both trekkers and Regina citizens on the grounds that the police had no motive for assaulting people and that such things just did not happen in Canada. "Stories of this kind are so improbable that we cannot accept them as in any way trustworthy."[63] The Commission did have to admit that a police assault took place, however, in the case of Reverend H. Upton, who was assaulted by a member of the RCMP. This was dismissed as an "accident." "A critical examination of the evidence convinces us that it was in all probability a pure accident. The fact was that Mr. Upton was running as fast as he could in one direction and encountered the end man of a squad of Mounted Police running in the opposite direction."[64]

The fighting continued off and on for well over two hours. The police relied mainly on baton charges with some use of tear gas and gunfire from service revolvers. The trekkers used mainly rocks but also makeshift clubs for combat at close quarters. Ronald Liversedge later described the scene as he remembered it in downtown Regina. "It was a terrible night, downtown Regina a shambles. Not a store with a window left in, the streets piled up with rocks and broken glass, dozens of cars piled up in the streets with no glass in them, and twisted fenders and bodies."[65]

By about 11 p.m. the main bodies of police ceased their baton charges and the fighting died down. The majority of the trekkers were then able to make for Exhibition Stadium. By now Detective Charles Millar of the Regina city police was dead, scores of trekkers, citizens and policemen were injured, and several trekkers and Regina citizens were hospitalized with gunshot wounds. Property damage to buildings and vehicles was in the tens of thousands of dollars.

195

Most of the trekkers had returned to their quarters at Exhibition Stadium by midnight. The RCMP then stationed men with rifles around the stadium and refused to allow anyone to leave. The trekkers were, in effect, imprisoned within the building, while the leaders and several of the rank and file who had been arrested before and during the rioting were held in the police station. There were also between 100 and 200 who did not return to the stadium and must have slept elsewhere in the city and surrounding countryside. Some probably left Regina permanently in the next day or two by catching freights individually or in small groups. With most of the strikers confined to the stadium without food or money, and many, including the leaders, under arrest elsewhere, the RCMP were firmly in control.

Premier Gardiner, who had been meeting with members of his cabinet to consider the trekkers' proposals when the rioting began, wired the prime minister late that night both protesting the police action and offering to disband the Trek under provincial auspices.

> They asked our Government to take responsibility for disbanding them to their own camps or homes. While we were meeting to consider their proposals and any suggestions we might make to you trouble started downtown between the police and strikers without notification to us of police intentions which has resulted in at least one death in the police force and scores of citizens, strikers and policemen wounded. We are nevertheless prepared to undertake this task of disbanding the men without sending them to Lumsden. Will you consider negotiations on basis of this proposal. [66]

This was the beginning of a dispute between the federal and provincial authorities on July 2 over the nature of the police action of the previous night and what to do about the trekkers now confined to Exhibition Stadium. The federal authorities at first refused to budge, insisting that the trekkers be fed only at Lumsden and disbanded from there. Gardiner was fearful that the intransigent federal attitude would lead to a resumption of hostilities at Exhibition Stadium and demanded that the federal authorities take a more reasonable position.

> Police intention to force these men to Lumsden camp or starving them into submission. This will end in a worse riot than last night. These men should be fed where they are and immediately disbanded and sent back to camps and homes as they request

without any attempt to force them into Lumsden and this should
be done within next two hours.[67]

After a further exchange of telegrams the federal government
relented sufficiently for Gardiner to initiate a process of negotiations
with the trekkers which resolved the immediate problem. It was
arranged to feed the men at the stadium and to register them with
the province for transportation to their homes or their original camps
as quickly as possible.[68] By July 4 the police guards were removed
from the exhibition grounds and the trekkers were allowed to eat
in city restaurants. On July 5 the trekkers departed for their homes
and camps in two special trains provided by the CNR and the CPR.
Fares and food allowances were provided by the Saskatchewan government who would later recoup the cost from Ottawa.

The expedition known as the On-to-Ottawa Trek, which had
begun in Vancouver on June 5, 1935, was now essentially over.
There were unsuccessful attempts to organize another trek from
points east of Regina. A few hundred men left Winnipeg but were
turned back by the RCMP before they reached Kenora, Ontario.
Eventually about 400 unemployed from various Ontario and Québec
localities did reach Ottawa in early August and camped in a city
park for a time. However, they did not receive much national
attention and their expedition was generally looked upon as anti-
climactic.

The Trek was over, but the trekkers had already written an
important chapter in Canadian history. And the political repercussions
were just beginning.

Footnotes

1. Public Archives of Canada (PAC), *McNaughton Papers,* Vol. 60, memorandum of telephone conversation between McNaughton and Brigadier
   Gordon, June 22, 1935.
2. *Ibid.,* Vol. 60, Wood to MacBrien, June 22, 1935.
3. *Ibid.,* Vol. 60, memorandum by McNaughton on instruction to be given
   DOC 12 by telephone, June 24, 1935.
4. *Ibid.*
5. House of Commons *Debates,* pp. 2899-3901, June 24, 1935.
6. *Ibid.*
7. *Ibid.*

8. RRIC *Exhibits,* Wood to MacBrien, June 24, 1935. Also reprinted in Victor Hoar (ed.), *Recollections of the On-to-Ottawa Trek* by Ronald Liversedge (McClelland and Stewart Ltd., 1973), pp. 221-226.

9. *Ibid.*

10. RRIC *Exhibits 14,* June 25, 1935. Also cited in Gladys Stone, "The Regina Riot: 1935," unpublished M.A. thesis, University of Saskatchewan, 1967, p. 66.

11. RRIC *Exhibits,* Wood to MacBrien, June 24, 1935. Also reprinted in Hoar, *op. cit.,* pp. 221-226.

12. RRIC *Exhibits,* Wood to MacBrien, June 25, 1935. Also reprinted in Hoar, *op. cit.,* pp. 226-228.

13. *Ibid.*

14. *Ibid.*

15. *Ibid.*

16. Stone, *op. cit.,* pp. 64-65.

17. *Ibid.*

18. RRIC *Exhibits,* Vol. I, p. 75.

19. *King Papers,* PAC, C 151593, Gardiner to Bennett, June 27, 1935.

20. *Ibid.,* C. 151591, Bennett to Gardiner, June 27, 1935.

21. RRIC Proceedings, Exhibits 200 and 209. Also cited in Stone, *op. cit.,* p. 69.

22. RRIC *Report,* Vol. I, p. 77. Also Evans, testimony to RRIC Proceedings and Regina *Leader-Post,* June 27, 1935, cited in Ben Swankey and Jean Evans Sheils, *Work and Wages: A Semi-Documentary Account of the Life and Times of Arthur H. (Slim) Evans, 1890-1944* (Vancouver: Trade Union Research Bureau, 1977), pp. 163-64.

23. Evans' testimony to RRIC Proceedings, cited in Swankey and Sheils, *op. cit.,* pp. 163-164. Two individuals, apparently representing Regina businessmen, made an anonymous donation of $500 and promised $500 more if the trekkers succeeded in hiring trucks to move out of the city.

24. RRIC *Exhibit 49,* MacBrien to Wood, June 27, 1935. Also cited in Stone, *op. cit.,* p. 72, and Swankey and Sheils, *op. cit.,* p. 165.

25. RRIC *Report,* Vol. I, p. 95.

26. Regina *Leader-Post,* June 28, 1935.

27. RRIC *Report,* Vol. I, pp. 96-97. This "phantom" order-in-council is also discussed in Stone, *op. cit.,* pp. 72-73, and Swankey and Sheils, *op. cit.,* pp. 167, 169.

28. RRIC *Report,* Vol. I, p. 95.

29. Stone, *op. cit.,* p. 73.

30. *Ibid.*

31. RRIC *Report,* Vol. I, p. 110.

32. Toronto *Daily Star,* June 29, 1935.

33. Robert Lipsett, "See 'Magna Carta' Scrapped by Bennett," Toronto *Daily Star,* June 29, 1935.

34. *Ibid.*

35. "Will Class All in Strike Body As Communists," Toronto *Daily Star*, June 29, 1935.
36. Grant Dexter, "Mystery in Ottawa Act to Halt Trek," Regina *Leader-Post*, June 29, 1935.
37. RRIC *Report*, Vol. I, p. 110.
38. *Ibid.*, pp. 110-111.
39. *Ibid.*, p. 80.
40. *Ibid.*
41. *Ibid.*, pp. 80-81.
42. RRIC *Report*, Vol. I, p. 81.
43. *Ibid.*, p. 111.
44. RRIC *Report*, Vol. I, p. 82.
45. *Ibid.*, p. 111.
46. Bagshaw and Leslie were prominent Saskatchewan Conservatives. Leopold was an old hand at prosecuting radicals. He had worked in Regina as an undercover agent posing as a house painter named Esselwein during the 1920s. He was at one time a delegate to the Regina Labour Council. Later he joined the Communist Party and became a confidante of the national leaders. A series of chance occurrences in 1927 and 1928 revealed Leopold as an RCMP agent and he dropped out of sight—being transferred to regular police duties in the Yukon. He reappeared in 1931 to supply much of the evidence used to convict Tim Buck and other Communist leaders under Section 98. Leopold was then assigned to office duties with the Security and Intelligence Branch and eventually achieved the rank of superintendent. He was also involved in the witch hunts and espionage trials surrounding the "Gouzenko affair" of 1946.
47. RRIC *Proceedings*, testimony by Assistant Commissioner Wood, reproduced in Swankey and Sheils, *op. cit.*, p. 177.
48. RRIC *Report*, Vol. I, pp. 117-118.
49. *Ibid.*, p. 118.
50. *Ibid.*, p. 81.
51. *Ibid.* For a fuller discussion of this point see Lorne Brown, "The Bennett Government, The Single Unemployed and Political Stability 1930-1935," unpublished Ph.D. thesis, Queen's University, 1979, pp. 473-477.
52. RRIC *Report*, Vol. I, pp. 113-115.
53. *Ibid.*
54. *Ibid.*, pp. 114-115.
55. *Ibid.*, p. 127.
56. RRIC *Proceedings*, Vol. 42, p. 62. Also cited in Stone, *op. cit.*, p. 83.
57. Regina *Daily Star*, July 2, 1935. Cited in Stone, *op. cit.*, p. 83.
58. Stone, *op. cit.*, p. 83.
59. RRIC *Report*, Vol. I, p. 127.
60. *Ibid.*, p. 115.
61. Hoar, *op. cit.*, p. 113.
62. RRIC *Report*, Vol. I, p. 148.

63. *Ibid.*, p. 149.
64. *Ibid.*
65. Hoar, *op. cit.*, p. 115.
66. *King Papers, op. cit.,* File 2119, C151584, Gardiner to Bennett, July 1, 1935.
67. *Ibid.,* File 2119, C1511585-86, July 2, 1935.
68. RRIC *Report*, Vol. I, p. 243.

CHAPTER XI

The Political Repercussions and the Legacy of the Trek

The immediate political results of the Regina Riot were extremely damaging to the Bennett government. The bitter relations between Regina and Ottawa worsened as Gardiner and his ministers continued to protest the violation of provincial jurisdiction over law enforcement. Over federal objections the Gardiner government appointed a commission of inquiry into the causes of the riot and the constitutional issues involved.

In the House of Commons the government came under bitter attack from the opposition and even criticism from some Conservative M.P.'s. But Bennett and his ministers stuck to their intransigent positions to the bitter end. Justice Minister Hugh Guthrie was put in the position of having to misrepresent the facts to the House of Commons.

> The attack was made in the first instance by the strike marchers, and the city police were called upon to defend themselves. Subsequently the mounted police joined for the purpose of maintaining order. Shots were exchanged. Shots were fired by the strikers and the fire was replied to by shots from the city police. [1]

Guthrie also claimed that the strikers had no legitimate grievances and that nearly half of them had never been in a relief camp. These charges were demonstrably false and this was pointed out by opposition spokesmen.

Prime Minister Bennett portrayed the Trek as "not a mere uprising against law and order but a definite revolutionary effort on the part of a group of men to usurp authority and destroy government."[2] He also charged that this attempt at revolution had been aided and abetted by CCF National Leader J.S. Woodsworth, Mayor McGeer of Vancouver, and Liberal Premier Pattullo of British Columbia.[3]

The attitudes and explanations of Bennett and his ministers outraged the opposition. Both CCF and Liberal spokespersons proclaimed that dragging out the "red bogey" was wearing thin and emphasized that the relief camps were obviously not working and should be replaced by a work and wages programme. Two Conservative back-benchers also criticized the camps and called for work and wages.[4]

One of the more eloquent attacks on the entire relief camp system was made by Agnes MacPhail of the CCF, Canada's first woman M.P. She declared that in view of the situation revolt was not only understandable but desirable.

> From the point of view of the future of Canada in my opinion it is much healthier to find that twenty thousand young men are restless to the point of revolt, after having been kept in camps from one to three years, than it would be if they were content. Why should one expect young, virile people, whether they be men or women, to be content with a life which at best gives food, provides work which may not be interesting, and for which there is no pay, and houses them in camps where all natural living and interest are denied? It is not reasonable to expect that they would be content with such a life, nor would it be healthy for Canada if they were.[5]

But the criticism in the House of Commons was mild compared to that leveled by municipal and provincial politicians. Mayor McGeer of Vancouver declared that "...the blood that has already flowed, and will again, forever remain on the head of the Prime Minister of Canada."[6]

One of the harshest criticisms was leveled by Attorney-General Arthur Roebuck of Ontario, who accused Bennett of creating a "red" scare and provoking the riot in an attempt to save the Conservatives from electoral defeat.

> Blood has flowed in the streets of Regina in order that the Conservative press may declare that our national life is at stake, and that Mr. Bennett is the saviour of the nation. To avoid defeat he would wade through slaughter to a throne and shut the gates of mercy on mankind.[7]

Roebuck also noted that there had been several "hunger marches" in Ontario in recent years with no violence or property damage and invited Bennett to stay out of Ontario in the interests of law and order.

During July and August 1935 the issues surrounding the Trek and the Regina Riot were kept before the public by trade unions and civil liberties associations. Large protest rallies were held in nearly every major city in the country immediately following the events of July 1. The Regina branch of the Citizens' Defence Committee was established on July 7 and in the succeeding weeks branches sprang up throughout the country. These committees sponsored public meetings, collected money, circulated petitions, and distributed leaflets and pamphlets.

More than 100 people had been arrested, most during the night of July 1. The charges included violation of Section 98, rioting, wounding, and assault. Of those charged with offences other than belonging to an unlawful association under Section 98, about half were released and the charges dropped within a few days. The charges against several others were dropped later, and, of those tried, only eight were convicted.[8] They were sentenced to prison terms ranging from seven to fifteen months. Nobody was ever charged in the death of Detective Charles Millar.

Of the eight people charged under Section 98, the charges against two were dropped and a third man was released at the preliminary hearing. Evans and four others were charged at the preliminary hearing and released on bail. The charges against all five were later withdrawn by Attorney-General Davis on the grounds that there was insufficient evidence to proceed.[9]

The outcome of the trials and the fact that in most cases the charges were withdrawn before trial—including all those charged under Section 98—was a moral victory for the trekkers and their supporters. It was also a political victory and a reflection of public opinion.

The relief camps, the Trek and the Regina Riot, and the plight of the unemployed in general were issues in the campaign leading up to the federal election of October 14, 1935. The Liberals, the CCF, and other opposition parties emphasized the issues of unemployment and mismanagement of the economy by the Bennett government. They promised to abolish the relief camps and institute a programme of work and wages. The question of the single unemployed was also linked to civil liberties issues and particularly Section 98 of the Criminal Code which the CCF, the Liberals and the Communists were all pledged to repeal. The Bennett government was already extremely unpopular among the majority of farmers, workers and small businessmen, even before the On-to-Ottawa Trek and the Regina Riot. In this sense it would be an exaggeration to claim that issues around the relief camps and civil liberties defeated the Conservatives. They would almost certainly have lost the 1935 election in any event. However, their handling of the Trek and the events in Regina symbolized to many voters what was wrong with the entire approach of the Bennett government.

Bennett was soundly defeated in the election with the Conservatives plummeting to forty seats—their lowest point since Confederation. They went from forty-nine per cent of the popular vote in 1930 to thirty per cent in 1935. The Tories were beaten especially severely in Western Canada and most particularly on the Prairies. They were elected in only one seat in Alberta, one in Saskatchewan and one in Manitoba. In Saskatchewan they declined from thirty-eight per cent to nineteen per cent of the vote—behind both the Liberals and the newly formed CCF.

The new Liberal government appointed the Rigg Committee to investigate and make recommendations concerning the relief camps. The committee recommended abolition of the camps, and the government began phasing them out in March 1936. On July 2, 1936, federal Labour Minister Norman Rogers announced that the last of the camps had closed and the federal relief camp system officially discontinued as of June 30. Some of the former relief camp inmates were given temporary jobs on railway construction and on farms but for most there was no permanent solution to the unemployment problem. The struggles of the single unemployed would be continued in the cities during 1936 and 1937 though they would never again become the focus of so much intense national attention. In 1936 Parliament also rescinded Section 98 of the Criminal Code which had been on the law books since the Winnipeg General Strike of 1919. The Relief Camp Workers' Union and their supporters could take much of the credit.

Those activists who built the Relief Camp Workers' Union and provided its primary and secondary leadership had accomplished a great deal since the onslaught of the Great Depression. They and their supporters agitated and organized first among the unemployed in the cities, and then in the camps. They worked with hardly any financial support and against great odds. And until at least 1934 they worked with few allies and very little support of any kind from the mainstream trade union movement and other mainstream economic and political institutions. They withstood some of the most severe state repression ever seen in Canada during peacetime. Perhaps most amazing of all, they had been one factor in changing the political psychology of the population from a public opinion which was generally reactionary and supportive of political repression in 1931 and 1932 to one which resisted that same repression in 1934 and 1935. The broader factors included the deprivations of the entire population and the fact that all levels of government were either unable or unwilling to take measures which would seriously alleviate the situation. The political outlook of Canadians was changing during the first half of the 1930s and the Bennett government was not keeping up with these changes.

By 1935 the public was demanding major reforms in the political system, as shown by the widespread and often enthusiastic support for the On-to-Ottawa Trek and by the overwhelming defeat of the Bennett government and the growth in support for radical and reform parties of many political stripes. Parties other than the Liberals and Conservatives received over twenty-five per cent of the popular vote in 1935 compared to six per cent in 1930.

The RCWU and its supporters had not accomplished these results by themselves. They were only one part of the political scene during the 1930s but they had played a crucial role in the process. How did they do it? There are no definitive answers to this question but a number of factors stand out. For the most part, RCWU activists were dedicated, self-educated working people. They were courageous and skillful in day-to-day struggle and no issue or grievance was too big or too small to demand their attention. They could operate effectively on a political stage as small as the smallest relief camp or as large as all of Canada. Their political judgement was usually sound and those who worked with them seldom questioned their devotion to the cause. They were not limited by the narrow confines of Parliamentary politics. They possessed ample quantities of both audacity and patience. They did not allow the powers that be to define what was legitimate and illegitimate in either political ideas or tactics and strategy. These activists earned the trust and respect and often the devotion first of the relief camp workers and later of countless thousands of the Canadian people.

The growth and rise to prominence of the RCWU did not happen spontaneously, although spontaneity did play an important role in the struggle. The RCWU was part of an organized, disciplined, dedicated and sophisticated left-wing movement which had deep roots among a significant minority of Canadian working people. They were the inheritors of a tradition of struggle stretching back into the nineteenth century.

Every generation of Canadian working people has produced activists and leaders who have learned from the past and struggled to achieve a better future. These are the activists who fought for the legalization of unions in 1872 and collective bargaining rights in the Winnipeg General Strike of 1919. They succeeded in abolishing the relief camps and extending civil liberties in 1936.

After 1935, hundreds of relief camp activists and those who worked with them played active roles in Canadian political struggles, and particularly the politics of the Canadian labour movement. Many were also active in the international political events of the late 1930s.

When the Mackenzie-Papineau Battalion was organized in 1937 to fight with the international brigades to defend democracy against fascism in the Spanish Civil War, the largest single response came from the veterans of the relief camps and the On-to-Ottawa Trek.[10] Scores of the rank and file and several of the RCWU leading activists went to Spain. One such Canadian was Paddy O'Neil, one of the many killed in Spain. Another was "Red" Walsh, a key organizer of the Trek and one of the eight leaders who met with the Bennett cabinet. Walsh continued to be a trade union activist when he returned to Canada. Another member of the brigades was Louis Tellier, a prominent French-Canadian activist with the RCWU. Ronald Liversedge, one of the leaders who would later write perhaps the most perceptive account of the relief camps and the Trek, also went to Spain. Canada sent more people per capita to the international brigades than any other country except France. Most would never return. Some who did fought later in World War II.

Many veterans of the RCWU and the Trek would be trade union activists for the rest of their lives. It could be said that the relief camps were the schools where they received their trade union and political educations. Louis Tellier, after fighting in Spain, became an activist in the Canadian Seamen's Union, which was especially active on the Great Lakes. Robert Jackson would become an activist and officer in the International Woodworkers of America (IWA) in British Columbia. Robert (Dusty) Miller would become an activist with the hard rock miners of Flin Flon, Manitoba. Irvine Schwartz was active in both the Canadian Seamen's Union and the IWA. Bill Gilbey was one of the founders of the RCWU and was active with the union until just before the On-to-Ottawa Trek when he managed to obtain a job in Vancouver. Gilbey would later be active with the needle trades in Manitoba and an official with the Grain Services Union in Saskatchewan. He became president of the Saskatchewan Federation of Labour in the 1960s. Robert (Doc) Savage got his nickname because he was adept at providing first aid to men in the relief camps. Later he was active with the Pulp and Paper Workers in B.C. Savage is today the last surviving member of the eight-man delegation which met Bennett in Ottawa.

These are only a few of the better known leading activists of the RCWU who were later active in Canadian trade union politics. They were not atypical: most people who experienced the relief camps and took part in the Trek were affected by the experience for life. For them the struggle did not end on that fateful day when the Trek met a violent end in Regina. They went on to help build the great CIO unions of the late 1930s, and veterans of the unemployed struggles could be found in the organizing drives of the automobile, steel, forestry, meat packing, and pulp and paper industries throughout Canada. They were also active in that broad movement which played a role in compelling governments to implement unemployment insurance, family allowances, old age security, and numerous other reforms which would eventually benefit the majority of ordinary Canadians.

In many ways Arthur (Slim) Evans provided the example. In 1937 he was a leader in the Medical Fund campaign for the Mackenzie-Papineau Battalion in Spain. In 1938 and 1939 Evans was a leader of the drive to organize the mining and smelting workers of Trail, B.C. He established a local of the Mine, Mill and Smelter Workers, which eventually succeeded in organizing the Consolidated Mining and Smelting Company in 1943.

In 1940 Evans got a job in the shipyards in Vancouver and soon became a shop steward of the Amalgamated Shipwrights. He worked in the shipyards until he was killed by a car in 1944. The hundreds who attended his funeral on a week day in Vancouver attest to his status. They were mainly working people of diverse national and racial origins. There were Chinese and Black people, East Indians and Native Indians, and no doubt people from backgrounds representing most of the countries of Europe. They reflected the mosaic which made up the workers of British Columbia and much of Canada.

The tributes to Evans emphasized his work in the labour movement, most particularly his work with the single unemployed.

And if you're looking for monuments to the man, go up along the CPR mainline and watch for those still standing tar papered shacks into which Bennett herded the unemployed youth of Canada back in those days. They're empty now, their windows boarded up, deserted for years. And Arthur Evans is the man who closed them down forever, so far as labour is concerned. [11]

Footnotes

1. House of Commons *Debates*, July 2, 1935.
2. *Ibid.*
3. *Ibid.*
4. *Ibid.*
5. *Ibid.*
6. Ben Swankey and Jean Evans Sheils, *Work and Wages: A Semi-Documentary Account of the Life and Times of Arthur H. (Slim) Evans, 1890-1944* (Vancouver: Trade Union Research Bureau, 1977), p. 204.
7. "Regina Riot was 'Planned' Says Roebuck," Toronto *Globe*, July 4, 1935.
8. Gladys Stone, "The Regina Riot: 1935," unpublished M.A. thesis, University of Saskatchewan, 1967, p. 89-90.
9. *Ibid.*, pp. 90-91.
10. Victor Hoar, *The Mackenzie-Papineau Battalion* (Toronto: The Copp Clark Publishing Company, 1969), pp. 25-30.
11. Charles Stewart, funeral address, "Hundreds Pay Final Tribute to Veteran Labour Leader," *The People*, Vancouver, February 19, 1944. Cited in Swankey and Sheils, *op. cit.*, p. 5.

Write for free catalogue of more than 110 books:

Black Rose Books
3981 boul. St. Laurent
Montréal, Québec
H2W 1Y5

Printed by
the workers of
Editions Marquis, Montmagny, Qué.
for
Black Rose Books Ltd.